# 54 Torah Talks

for Barbara at Mesh
love
Brian

# 54 Torah Talks:

✦

## From Layperson To Layperson

*Brian Weinstein*

iUniverse, Inc.
New York   Bloomington

## 54 Torah Talks
### From Layperson to Layperson

iUniverse books may be ordered through booksellers or by contacting:

iUniverse
1663 Liberty Drive
Bloomington, IN 47403
www.iuniverse.com
1-800-Authors (1-800-288-4677)

Because of the dynamic nature of the Internet, any Web addresses or links contained
in this book may have changed since publication and may no longer be valid.

ISBN: 978-1-4401-9253-1 (sc)
ISBN: 978-1-4401-9254-8 (dj)
ISBN: 978-1-4401-9255-5 (ebk)

Printed in the United States of America

iUniverse rev. date: 01/13/2010

*Thanks to Dr. Morris J. Levitt*

# Contents

# *Preface*

Almost every Friday for the last ten years I have made a telephone call to my colleague and friend from Howard University, Dr. Morris J. Levitt, to talk about the Parashah or Torah reading for the week. I was preparing a short presentation to the congregation attending the Kabbalat Shabbat service at Adas Israel, a Conservative Jewish congregation in Washington, DC. The cantors, first Maurice Singer and then Jenna Greenberg, permitted me to speak. Every few months I prepared a longer talk for the Shabbat morning Egalitarian Minyan at Adas Israel. This book is a combination of the short and the long talks.

In addition to Dr. Levitt, my friends Richard Spero and Rabbi Dr. Yosef Green read drafts of these longer remarks. As a layperson, who did not benefit from a traditional Jewish education, I needed all the help I could get. Rabbi Dr. Green, an extraordinary pulpit rabbi in Jerusalem and an important biblical scholar, gently encouraged me to pursue ideas with which he did not always agree. A single word from him, a single bibliographic reference sent me down a new path of inquiry. Rabbi Dr. Morris Faierstein, teacher and highly respected American scholar of Jewish mysticism and of the history of the Yiddish language, advised me to publish with iUniverse and took the time from his own research to help me resolve important questions. Nina Graybill, Esq. read the text and offered suggestions. Ms. Heeral Trivedi, a contemporary Indian artist, took time from the preparation of her new solo show to paint a watercolor for the cover of this book.

These 54 commentaries or *drashot* were better because of all these interactions. Of course, I bear full responsibility for any failings in this text.

For transliteration, Hebrew to English, I have tried to follow the new Jewish Publication Society translation of the Bible. Citations from the Talmud, Midrash, and rabbinic classic commentaries follow the standard editions.

# Introduction

At first reading, no book, secular or holy, is more intimidating than the Torah, the first five books of the Jewish Bible or *Tanakh* (T for Torah, law; N for *Nevi'im*, prophets; K for *Ketuvim*, writings). The stories, many of the commandments, and the context often seem perplexing and alien to us moderns. In addition, what could a layperson say that had not been said before by the sages of the oral Torah, the Talmud, the countless classical rabbinic commentators such as Rashi, Nachmanides, and Abraham Ibn Ezra, modern biblical scholarship, and sermons, books and articles, and *responsa* or discussions and answers to contemporary questions?

I started with the simple premise that reading and thinking about holy texts is at the heart of Jewish identity for laypersons as well as for scholars and clergy. We all must study to be fully Jewish. Although study is its own reward, why not share one's thoughts with others? What better place to study and share than at the daily and Shabbat services? I concluded that anyone with an idea about the weekly portion and the willingness to read further to add depth and analysis could speak briefly to other laypeople. But, where would those ideas come from? Thanks to the organization of the Torah, this task proved to be much easier than expected. It only took some time.

Since the Torah is divided into fifty-four sections or Parashot, each Parashah is short enough to permit frequent readings. I decided to be quite passive and to relax. After the third or fourth reading of one Parashah an idea would jump out of the text at me. Something interesting, strange, beautiful, contradictory, or even shocking demanded further study. The sages of the Talmud, Rashi and the other commentators almost always had something to say. When they were silent, that too was interesting to me. Based on the Torah and the commentary, I could try to think of a contemporary application. I used my training in the social sciences to do more research into history, archaeology, politics, sociology and language.

Because of my own experiences and biases, certain themes in my approach to the study of the Torah have emerged. (It was only when Dr. Levitt pointed out these themes to me that I realized it.) They give some unity to this book.

1. The Torah is a source of Jewish identity, direction and civility.
2. The sages, rabbis, judges and intellectuals have great moral authority in Judaism. They must be studied in connection with Torah study because they help guide the community. The Talmud is essential for an understanding of the Torah.
3. We study the Torah to improve the quality of our existence in the here and now and constantly to renew our relationship with the Almighty. There is nothing irrelevant about the Torah.
4. Jews do not live isolated from other peoples. Jews must get along with them, no matter what their beliefs and practices are.
5. Jews respect other nations and are open to learn from them.
6. Jews try to remember the maligned and those who live on the periphery. The seemingly minor persons in the Torah should be studied. They are in the Torah for a reason.
7. Egalitarianism, meaning inclusiveness of men and women in our prayer services, is an important principle for me. God transcends gender, but I refer to the Almighty as "He" in this book because the Torah text consistently uses this pronoun.
8. Jewish law and custom evolve to fit contemporary needs, even as we struggle to maintain our commitment to *Halakhah*, Jewish law. This principle reflects our belief that God recognizes we have free will: we choose, we act, we argue among ourselves; we evolve intellectually and spiritually.
9. Jews have a forward looking perspective even though we study intensely our past. We learn from the past, but we live in the present and plan for the future. As much as we may hope in the coming of the Messiah and the subsequent redemption, most of us do not dwell on these promises. Jews are very much part of the world as it is and as we hope it to be.
10. We recognize that animal and grain sacrifices at the Temple in Jerusalem where the sacrifices took place, were important for our ancestors, but most of us do not anticipate or look forward to their restoration. Although some prayers express hope for the restoration of the Temple in Jerusalem, the possibility of that ever happening is remote. Muslims, who had nothing to do with the destruction of the Temple, have built important and beautiful sanctuaries on the site of the Temple, and they must be respected.
11. Israel is central to our identity. God promised us this land, and its survival is important for the safety of the Jewish people worldwide. There is no contradiction between love for Israel and love for the countries, such as the United States of America, where many of us live. All humans have multiple identities, and they can be loyal to all of them.

12. Jews must survive as part of God's plan for the universe. Jews are witnesses to the One God; we record and communicate His greatness and supremacy to the world.
13. We respect our scholars from the past and the present. They are central to the process of teaching and study. They guide us, but we do not always have to agree with them.
14. Laypersons like me should be encouraged to study and to express their questions and opinions for all to discuss.

It is important to say clearly, and at the start, that this book is not meant to be a running commentary on the Torah. For that we have countless *Chumashim*, the term used for the Torah in book form, in many different languages which have been published over the centuries. We have separate commentaries in books and articles written by great sages, rabbis and scholars. Rather, each of the 54 chapters in my book is based on one or two points that came to me, a layperson, while reading the text. This approach sometimes means that the main subject of a particular Parashah is barely mentioned, if at all. Thus, I say practically nothing about the giving of the commandments on Mount Sinai in Parashat *Yitro* because what came out of the text to me was *Yitro*, the person. I could not stop thinking about him despite the momentous events in the portion named after him. Another disappointment to readers may be the absence of commentary on the Torah readings for the festivals. They are obviously important, but I decided to focus only on the 54 weekly Parashot.

Other laypersons will find different points of interest in each Parashah, and they may ask "Why didn't Weinstein deal with that subject?" This means they have found something important for them; they must pursue their own questions, impressions and ideas by reading and re-reading the text (four times is a good start) and seeking comments by the scholars and sages.

Originality is not the point. The point is to study for its own sake and to share with others if possible. In the Jewish tradition intellectual passivity is not a virtue.

# B'REISHIT/GENESIS

# 1

## B'reishit

✦

### *(Genesis 1:1 – 6:8)*

Have you ever started reading a book by turning the pages to the conclusions after getting an idea of the contents? If there is a happy ending, our anxiety is lower; if the authors conclude by satisfactorily answering questions they have raised at the beginning, then we can read contentedly through the anticipated trials and tribulations.

A quick glance at the end of the Torah, Parashat *V'zot ha-B'rakhah,* is not reassuring. The events we read about are sad and seemingly disconnected from *B'reishit.* The Israelites are weeping for Moses, who has just died, whereas in the first Parashah we celebrate the creation of the earth. The actors are different; the places are far from each other; and God's purposes seem inconsistent. Reading the end is thus disconcerting; we don't seem to have much to look forward to.

I believe there are three interconnected themes which unite the last chapters of this holy text with the first chapters, meaning there is consistency. First, the uses and misuses of human intelligence; second, exile and return from exile; and third, the loss and rediscovery of intimacy with God. Although this first chapter of the book is, of course, a commentary on the first Parashah of the Torah, I want to look for a moment at the last Parashah:

*V'zot ha B'rakhah* means "This is the Blessing," and it refers to Moses' last message to the Israelites which includes his blessing. His words are God's words because we are reminded that Moses, who wrote the Torah on God's instructions and "whom the Lord singled out face to face " (Deut 34:10) was more intimate with God than was any other human being.

During the few hours remaining to him, Moses reminds Israel of God's message from Sinai; he lovingly blesses each tribe and summarizes their relationship with God, concluding with a promise of well-being for Israel in the Promised Land. He climbs to the top of Mount Nebo where God shows him the Promised Land.  He breathes his last and dies at the age of 120. (Deut 34:7) No one else in the Torah dies at that age, as far as I know, even though in Parashat *B'reishit* we read that God says 120 is the proper age to die. (Gen 6:3)

After Moses' death the Almighty tells us that Israel's leader used his intelligence to serve God. Moses dealt with the King of Egypt, and he displayed "might and awesome power...before all Israel." (Deut 34:10-12) Moses organized and led all the tribes of Israel. He taught the laws of God, thereby freeing his people from idolatry. The people were intelligent. Otherwise, they never would have understood the nature of the Covenant. Moses had recognized the strength of their minds: "Surely, this Instruction [i.e. the Torah] which I enjoin upon you this day is not too baffling for you, nor is it beyond reach." (Deut 30:11) The great medieval commentator, Ibn Ezra (Rabbi Abraham ben Meir ibn Ezra 1089 – 1164), said "intelligence is the basis of the Torah. The Torah was not given to ignoramuses. Man's intelligence is the angel which mediates between him and his God." (Ibn Ezra, "Introduction," to Genesis, p. 10)

We learn the source of this intelligence and how humans use and misuse it from *B'reishit*: "God created man in His image...." (Gen 1:27). This sentence cannot mean that humans look like God because the Almighty has no particular form. Maimonides (Rabbi Moses ben Maimon or Rambam 1135-1204) wrote that the phrase "in His image" means that humanity was given "Divine intellect" and "intellectual perception." (*The Guide*, p.14)

Next, we read in the first Parashah of the Torah that God gives human beings power, a force for their intelligence to use, by decreeing that they "shall rule...the whole earth." (Gen 1:26) and shall choose names for all the animals and plants. Emboldened by their power, Adam and his new partner, Eve, want more. The serpent promises them the ultimate in knowledge and power: eat from the tree of knowledge of good and bad and "you will be like divine beings." (Gen 3:5) Despite the Lord's explicit warning to avoid the tree, they succumb to the serpent's words.

Immediately after tasting the fruit "they perceived that they were naked" (Gen 3:7) meaning that intelligent persons know themselves first. God forestalls Adam's and Eve's growing arrogance by expelling them before they can eat from another tree in the garden, namely, the tree of life. With intelligence, knowledge, power plus eternal life they would have threatened God's sovereignty over the universe.

As Adam and Eve depart into exile, "[s]ome natural tears they dropped but wiped them soon; The world was all before them, where to choose Their place of rest, and Providence their guide; They hand in hand with wand'ring steps and slow, Through Eden took their solitary way." These are Milton's words from *Paradise Lost*. (Milton, Book XII: 645) Expulsion and a search for a place to rest is the beginning of human history, a chronicle of our deeds and misdeeds, the uses and misuses of our intelligence. God seems to abandon Adam and Eve who must make a new life in the harsh world outside the idyllic garden.

In comparison, God perceives a similar threat from Moses. After the exodus from Egypt the people demand water at *Meribath-Kadesh*. God tells Moses exactly how to obtain water, but Moses speaks loudly to a rock while striking it with his staff thus giving the impression that he himself is performing the miracle without any heavenly assistance. (Milgrom, p. 454) The Lord punishes his presumptuousness by forbidding him to enter the Promised Land. God does not, however, abandon Moses because Moses must continue to lead and to teach.

In Parashat *B'reishit* God blocks humanity's return to Eden by stationing "east of the garden...the cherubim and the fiery ever-turning sword...." (Gen 3:24) Eden does not disappear. God is, in fact, preserving this garden for later generations who will receive and obey His commandments. When Moses dies, we read in the Talmud (T'murah 16a) that he goes into the Garden of Eden.

Moses' entry into Eden represents more than a return to a specific geographic location; he is entering into that special intimate relationship with God which had been lost by Adam and Eve. Moses must sense what this means as when near his death he tells his people: "God is a refuge. A support are the arms everlasting." (Deut 33:27-28). Moses is thinking he will embrace and be embraced by the Almighty.

The details of Moses' death make this idea of embracing more clear: "So Moses the servant of the Eternal died there in the land of Moab, according to the word of the Eternal." (Deut 34:5) The Hebrew for "according to the word of the Eternal" is *al pi Adonai* which Rashi (Rabbi Shlomo Yitzchaki, 1040-1105) translates as "by the mouth of the Lord" meaning that God kisses Moses taking Moses' breath or spirit or soul from his mouth. (Rashi on Deut 34:5) Talmud calls this the "divine kiss." (Mo'ed Katan 28a) This should remind us of *B'reishit* when God touches Adam in a similarly intimate way by blowing into Adam's "nostrils the breath of life, and man became a living being." (Gen 2:7. Cf. Onkelos, p.10 ftn. 7)

Adam and Eve originally lived in close proximity with God: "And they heard the sound of the Lord God walking in the garden...." (Gen 3:8) When the first humans are sent into exile, God also departs from the garden into the heavens. Subsequent Parashot beginning with *No-ach* tell us how later generations disappoint God.

After destroying most of the earth in the great flood the Almighty decides He will make an agreement or Covenant with one family founded by Abraham and Sarah. He will count on this family to obey and worship Him, the one and only God. Their descendants will learn about the Covenant and God's laws from a man called Moses. God promises in the Book of Leviticus that if this family obeys the laws, God will finally return to earth. "I will walk among you [as He did in Adam and Eve's garden]; I will be God to you and you will be a people to me" (Lev 26:12)

What does all this mean to us living, as we do, outside of Eden? The closest we can get to God is through His teaching, transmitted to us through Moses in the form of the Torah and also transmitted to us through the sages of the oral Torah or Talmud.

Before reading and studying the Torah in a synagogue prayer service we kiss it as it is carried around the room and when we approach it to say the prayer. Zohar, the great mystical text, explains that "kissing represents the cleaving of spirit to spirit." (Zohar, Vol II:124b) When the Kohen is called for the first reading from the Parashah of the week, the *gabbai* or lay volunteer leader says: "Blessed be He who in His holiness gave the Torah to His people Israel." The congregants respond: "And you, who cleave unto the Lord your God, are alive every one of you this day." As the Torah scroll is returned to the ark, Jews sing God's words "Forsake not My Torah. It is a Tree of Life to them that hold fast to it...." (Proverbs 4:2, 3:18) We embrace the scroll in place of God who since the Garden of Eden is separate from our communities.

This idea of separation is central to the story of creation in Parashat *B'reishit*: Separation of the sky from the earth; humanity from other living things; brother from brother; alienation of humanity from God. In subsequent chapters of the Torah God volunteers a way for reconciliation of humanity with God. And, in the last Parashah, *V'zot ha-B'rakhah*, the "end of the story," the Master of the Universe promises that our intelligence can lead us to obey the laws as transmitted by Moses. Obedience ensures that we shall return to live with God in the Garden of Eden. In the *Yizkor* or Memorial Service for the deceased we express the hope that after death our souls are "bound up in the bond of life among the souls of...the patriarchs and matriarchs, and all the righteous men and women in the Garden of Eden."

Thus, we begin to study the Torah with confidence that Torah is a cohesive whole from the first Parashah, *B'reishit*, to the last, *V'zot ha-B'rakhah*. For me it is also important to know that the story beginning with the expulsion of Adam and Eve from their land has a happy ending with God's embrace of Moses and the people of Israel returning finally to their Promised Land.

# 2

## *No-ach*

✦

## *(Genesis 6:9-11:32)*

Because of the misbehavior of the descendants of Adam and Eve, God destroys almost all living things on the planet with a great flood. Because of *No-ach's* righteousness, he and his family along with pairs of earthly animals will be saved within an ark. When the waters subside after forty days and nights of rain, a second process of creation will begin with No-ach's family and the creatures that emerge on dry land from the ark.

God gives No-ach, who is grateful for his life, commandments meant as guidelines for all human behavior. God also promises not to destroy the earth again. To seal this covenant with the new progenitor of humanity God places a rainbow in the sky for all to see.

Humanity and the animal kingdom proliferate. We read the genealogies of the peoples who begin to repopulate the earth. Shem, a son of No-ach, will be the ancestor of Abram (later to be called Abraham), but Abram's importance is not evident as yet. Everything seems fine until a unified and arrogant humanity has the idea to build a tower "with its top in the sky, to make a name for ourselves" (Gen 11:4) God perceives this action as a threat to His sovereignty and disperses humanity to the ends of the earth where they develop their different languages which disunite them.

Through the details about No-ach, the ark, the flood, the regeneration of humankind and the very detailed genealogies God is sending us several messages. Among these messages are the following:

1.  Pay attention to numerical references. The ark of No-ach must be 300 cubits long, 50 cubits wide and 30 cubits high. Much later we learn that the Temple in Jerusalem must be 50 cubits wide and 30 cubits high. The dimensions of the Holy Ark and other objects are very specific. This shows us that God always demands precision.

7

2.  Recognize the concept of Covenant, an agreement or contract between God and the people. God commits to preserving the earth, but humanity must obey the commandments. In the next Parashah God refines this concept with Abram's/Abraham's and his and Sarai's/Sarah's descendants.

3.  Understand the concept of *kashrut* which means fit for human consumption, from which we get the word kasher/kosher. God explains that the blood of an animal is not fit. There are pure and impure animals which God will elaborate eventually.

4.  Observe the repetition of words and concepts. The ark of No-ach is called in Hebrew a *tebah*. The only other reference to a *tebah* in Torah is the container or basket into which the baby Moses is placed by his mother. Jews from Iraq call the ark which contains the Torah in their synagogues the *tebah*. This indicates that the ark of No-ach saves humanity; so, too, the ark of Moses, who will lead Israel out from Egyptian slavery; the ark within the synagogue preserves God's teaching, the Torah, so that Jews may learn about the Covenant and survive as a people.

5.  Dwell on the commandments. God prohibits murder, albeit not so explicitly as in Parashat *Yitro* in the Book of Exodus. This is the introduction to the many rules of behavior we shall learn throughout the Torah. Altogether, these are the important underlying messages in this Parashah.

From time to time a mission of exploration tries to find remains of No-ach's ark. What a colossal waste of time and money! God's transcendent message is what counts, not finding some archaeological remains. God has been disappointed with humankind ever since Adam and Eve disobeyed Him. He is reconciled to humanity's deficiencies and decides to let them live. God develops a plan which includes giving people rules about how to live, and how to behave toward Him and toward other human beings. God's disappointment with humanity as a whole leads Him to conclude that He must choose a people with the singular responsibility to teach His message to everyone else.

Parashat *B'reishit* and Parashat No-ach are together a type of foreword to God's book, the Torah.

# 3

## *Lekh L'kha*

✦

## *(Genesis 12:1-17:27)*

"And the Lord said to Abram, 'Go forth [*lekh l'kha*] from your land and your birthplace and your father's house to the land I will show you. And I will make of you a great nation and I will bless you and make your name great and you shall be a blessing.'" (Gen 12:1-2). These words begin to define the particular history and characteristics of the Jewish religion and Jewish people. The two words themselves, *lekh l'kha*, raise two questions: Go forth from where? Why go forth? The answers help explain the origins and the importance of the separate and distinctive identity of the Jews:

### Go Forth From Where?

Abram's native land and his father's house are in Ur and in Haran located in Mesopotamia, an area encompassing historical Assyria, Sumeria and Babylonia. At least 1500 years after Abram the Jews are once again in Ur and Haran where they have been involuntarily brought by the conquering Babylonians. King Cyrus, the Persian king who conquered Babylonia, tells them: "The Lord God of Heaven has given me all the Kingdoms of the earth, and has charged me with building Him a House in Jerusalem, which is in Judah. Any one of you of all His people, the Lord his God be with him and let him go up." (II Chron 36:23) Thus, Abram's departure from Babylon is not definitive.

What seems to be the recurring departure from Babylon differs from the single exodus from Egypt that we read about in the Book of Exodus. The two departures from Babylon- that of Abram and that of the Jews in the 6th century BCE - define Jews in a way different from the way departure from Egypt defines Jews. Egypt was a place of slavery, and departure, once and for all, meant freedom. In contrast, one thinks about the ancient and enduring

Jewish connections with Mesopotamia starting with Abram and the three matriarchs, Sarah, Rebecca and Rachel, as well as their handmaidens Bilhah and Zilpah, who were born there. Jonah was forced to preach in Nineveh, the capital of Assyria. Israelites were deported to Assyria in the 8th century BCE; the Judahites were deported to Babylonia in the 6th century BCE.

Jeremiah advised Jews in Babylonian exile to make the most of their stay: "Multiply there, do not decrease. And seek the welfare of the city to which I have exiled you and pray to the Lord on its behalf, for in its prosperity you shall prosper." (Jer 29:4-7). But, the Psalmist tells us not to forget our origins: "By the rivers of Babylon there we sat and wept as we thought of Zion." (Psalm 137:1)

Even after Cyrus' initiative to encourage the Jews to return to Jerusalem, many Jews remained and made important contributions to Jewish history within Babylonia. The great sages of the Talmud preached and wrote in Babylonia. During the Muslim and Arab ascendancy scholars like Saadia Gaon (Saadia ben Joseph, CE 892-942) who migrated from Egypt, wrote, translated and taught in Mesopotamia. Travelers like Benjamin of Tudela found only a few hundred Jews in Jerusalem in the 12th century while many thousands lived in Baghdad with their academies and many synagogues. (Cf. Adler, pp. 38-63) A significant Jewish population remained in Iraq, the modern state in Mesopotamia, until shortly after the establishment of the State of Israel in 1948.

What this history shows is that although God and King Cyrus told Abram and the Jews to go out of Babylonia or Mesopotamia, they did not do so completely. Not all Jews were convinced of the need to depart from this land.

## Why Go Forth?

In light of the very long time Jews lived in Babylon, wouldn't it have been easier for Abram and his descendants to become the Chosen People without leaving their ancestral homeland? The answer is no, and the reason for it is found in the previous Parashah, No-ach.

We remember that humankind is reborn after the great flood which killed all of humanity except for the family of No-ach. Suddenly after the detailed genealogy of the new peoples of the earth we read the story of the Tower of Babel (Gen 11:1-9). It does not appear to be related to the context, but it is essential to understand the call to Abram to go out from Mesopotamia. Why?

Alarmed at the arrogance of humanity in wishing to build a tower to heaven, God "confounded their speech" so they could not communicate effectively among themselves and "scattered them from there over the face of the earth." After this punishment God calls on Abram to leave. The building of the tower and God's reaction to this human initiative are an answer to the question why Abram must depart.

The key to an understanding of *"lekh l'kha"* is the Hebrew word for "confound" as in God "confounded their speech." The root of the word is *beit-lamed-lamed*. Cognate and thus related words from this root are "mixture," "confusion," and "assimilation." In this sense, being assimilated means being part of a confused mixture. In short, the Almighty wants Abram to separate himself and his descendants from the confused mixture of peoples resulting from the destruction of the Tower of Babel. Separation means going out, leaving Babylon for a new land where Abram's name will be changed to Abraham and where he will be party to a new Covenant with God.

The second answer to the question "why leave?" comes from an analysis of God's words *lekh l'kha*. What is so special about the verb *lalekhet* which simply means "to go?" The root of the verb is *hei-lamed-khaf*. Cognate words built on the root and thus related to "to go" are "traveler," "walking," and "direction one is taking," "the way one is going," and "the way of going" which in Hebrew is *halakhah*. (Schaechter-Haham, pp. 151-152) *Halakhah* is the word for Jewish law. Separating from others and going out in a certain direction means observing a new law, *halakhah*.

What can we conclude from the foregoing? God orders the ancestors of Israel to go out and to separate themselves from other peoples. As the history of the Jews in Babylon shows, however, Jews have not departed from the various incarnations of Babylon *qua* dominant states in the world. Jews living outside the Land of Israel have been important contributors to their countries as scientists, artists, musicians, politicians, writers and intellectuals, entrepreneurs and athletes.

Today the spirit of Babylon lives in the Jews. This means that even Israeli Jews live in Babylon insofar as they participate fully in the modern world of science and culture.

The dilemma – going out but not really going out – is resolved by separating and belonging at the same time. Jews obey God's order *lekh l'kha* by following *halakhah* as much as possible no matter where they live. This means keeping a kosher home, keeping the Shabbat, studying, charity, prayer, maintaining close ties to Israel. Jews participate fully and are loyal to secular societies and governments everywhere in the world.

Jewish history shows that Jews can and do belong to two worlds by building homes in Babylon while not forgetting Jerusalem.

# 4

## *Va-yera*

✦

## *(Genesis 18:1-22:24)*

After the Almighty "appeared" (*va-yera*) through angels to Abraham (whose name God changed from Abram – Gen 17:5) he understands that his wife Sarah (whose name was changed from Sarai – Gen 17:15) would give birth. Within a year Isaac is born, and he is circumcised as God instructed on the eighth day as a sign of the Covenant. (Gen 21:4) Despite the fact Isaac is the second son of Abraham, he is preeminent. Ishmael, the first born of Abraham and son of Hagar, the maid, and also circumcised according to God's instructions, will be excluded from the Covenant between Abraham and God. Eventually both Ishmael and his mother Hagar will be excluded from Abraham's home. Should we ignore Ishmael?

As Isaac grows up Sarah becomes alarmed that Ishmael might threaten Isaac's succession to his father. Sarah finds a solution when she forces her husband to expel Hagar and Ishmael into the wilderness. God appears to Hagar and promises that she and her offspring will survive and thrive. Ishmael is destined to become the ancestor of "a great nation." (Gen 21:18) Abraham would be happy to know about this prediction because he loves his firstborn having pleaded with God not to forget the young man: "O that Ishmael might live by Your favor." (Gen 17:18)

Ishmael reappears in the Bible, and Jews have had both positive and negative attitudes about him and his descendants, the Arabs. Ibn Ezra says that after Sarah's death Abraham reestablished contact with Ishmael sending presents to Ishmael's twelve children. (Ibn Ezra, on Gen 21:14) The Torah tells us that Ishmael returned many years after the events in this Parashah to help Isaac bury their father in Hebron. Ishmaelites (or Midianites) also reappear in the story of Joseph when they purchase Joseph from his brothers and carry him to Egypt. Josephus writes (*Ant.* I.10.4) that Ishmaelites were the famous Nabateans of the Negev Desert, and he refers to them as a virtuous and dignified Arab people. Ramban (Nachmanides, Rabbi Moshe ben Nachman, 1194/1195-circa 1270), on the other hand, says Sarah had good reason to demand the expulsion of Ishmael because he had shot arrows at her son Isaac and because he was worshipping idols. (Ramban on Gen 21:9)

The Arab and Muslim view of Ishmael is quite different even though the influence of the Hebrew Bible is evident. According to the Koran, "Yet before it [the Koran] the Book of Moses was revealed, a guide and a blessing to all men. This Book confirms it." (Sura 46:12) S.D. Goitein, preeminent scholar of Jewish and Muslim relations asserts that "The Jewish notion that the Arabs are Ishmaelites and hence the descendants of Ishmael, the son of Abraham, was taken over by the Arabs themselves." (Goitein, *The Jews and Arabs,* p. 22) In the Arab-Muslim view, Ishmael was chosen as a prophet, and Muslims seem to believe that it was Ishmael, not Isaac, whom Abraham was going to sacrifice on God's command. The sacrifice was going to take place in Mecca, they believe, and Abraham and Ishmael built in Mecca the *Ka'aba* or *Bayt Allah*, the most holy structure in the Islamic world. (Sura 2:125-127)

The story of Ishmael in the Hebrew Bible is one of several examples of the rejection of primogeniture. By the rules of primogeniture the first born – usually the son – succeeds the father as head of the family, clan, tribe or nation. This seems to be an almost universal principle.

Other examples of the rejection of the firstborn are: Jacob over Esau, Judah over Reuben, and Jacob's blessing of his grandson Ephraim over Ephraim's older brother Manassah. "When Joseph saw that his father was placing his right hand on Ephraim's head, he thought it wrong; so he took hold of his father's hand to move it from Ephraim's head to Manassah's. 'Not so, father,' Joseph said to his father, 'for the other is the first-born, place your right hand on his head.'" Jacob responds: "I know my son, I know. He too shall become a people, and he too shall be great. Yet his younger brother shall be greater than he...." (Gen 48:13-19)

In this Parashah there are other types of behavior that seem contrary to nature and logic. We read that strangers – probably angels – who previously visited Abraham and Sarah, travel to the home of Lot, Abraham's nephew, who was living in Sodom. Lot protects these visitors from the unruly mob who are demanding to use them for their sexual gratification. Lot offers his own young unmarried daughters to the mob: "You may do to them as you please, but do not do anything to these men, since they have come under the shelter of my roof." (Gen 19:8)

Lot's astounding decision shows the dichotomy between tradition and choice. By tradition Lot has an obligation to protect his family, but he chooses to protect his visitors. Fortunately for the daughters, the angelic visitors blind the mob, and the town is soon destroyed. As in the choice of Isaac over Ishmael, the tradition is violated.

A last example is God's instruction to Abraham that he sacrifice his son Isaac who was supposed to succeed his father. This is a strange and frightening demand even though we eventually realize that God is testing Abraham's obedience.

The message is that the Almighty is not bound by what humans consider to be "normal."

He often acts contrary to what one might think is "natural" or "traditional." He chooses Canaan as the Promised Land rather than Mesopotamia where Abraham and Sarah already live. This couple should have had children when they were young, but they had Isaac when Sarah was well beyond her biological childbearing age. The vigorous effort by Sarah to promote her son and to exclude Ishmael is unexpected and curious in a patriarchal society. Similarly, male circumcision changes the natural form of the body. Rules of kashrut that are made more explicit later in the text seem quite arbitrary.

At the beginning of the covenantal relationship between God and the Israelites God is saying there is no natural or expected reason for His choice of Abraham and his descendants as partners. He is being arbitrary, for God is not governed by nature or tradition. Just before the Israelites cross the Jordan River into the Promised Land Moses dispels any notion that the Israelites are better than anyone else: "know, then that it is not for any virtue of yours that the Lord your God is giving you this good land to possess." (Deut 9:6) The truth of the matter is that God could have chosen someone else as His people. It could have been Ishmael and his descendants, for example.

The message in this text is that God has a plan which Jews must try to understand and follow. We understand that we shall not find the plan in nature, tradition or intuition; we shall find it in the Tanakh or Bible, the Talmud or rabbinic commentary, and Midrash or interpretation of the Bible. We must study these texts. Serious study and observance of the commandments do not mean isolation from the natural world and from other peoples. On the contrary, the descendants of Abraham and Sarah live among others in the modern world. They remember that God spoke to Hagar and that Abraham also loved his first son, Ishmael.

# 5

## *Chayyei Sarah*

✦

### *(Genesis 23:1-25:18)*

Thinking about the death and burial of Sarah, the first matriarch, focuses the mind on the role of women in the Torah. The text begins: "Sarah's lifetime [*Chayyei Sarah*] came to one hundred and twenty-seven years. Sarah died in Kiriath-arba…." (Gen 23:1-2) This reads like the beginning of an obituary.

In this chapter I want to complete Sarah's obituary. My purpose is to suggest that once we realize how important she was, we shall agree with those who wish to include her name in the beginning of the Amidah prayer, the central prayer of every daily and Sabbath Jewish prayer service which traditionally only recognizes the three patriarchs.

### An Obituary for Sarah

Abraham, son of Terah, has announced the sudden death of his beloved wife, Sarah, aged 127, in Kiriath-arba, in the Land of Canaan. The cause of death was not indicated, but false rumors about the death of her only beloved son, Isaac, might have broken her heart. The family, recent arrivals in the area of Hebron, have been well-regarded by the local Hittite inhabitants. A leading member of that community, Ephron, son of Zohar, sold them land with the Machpelah cave for a family burial site. There she was laid to rest.

Sarah, like her husband, was born into the family of Terah in the town of Ur in southern Mesopotamia. She married her husband whose name at the time was Abram. She was the granddaughter of Terah and the daughter of Haran, Abraham's brother. People called her Sarai, which means my princess; God changed her name to Sarah which means "princess over all" (Rashi, on Gen 17:15) These names are titles probably referring to her great beauty and dignity. Talmudic sources tell us that her real name was Iscah, meaning to foresee. (Sanhedrin 69b) Altogether these names suggest a strong and intelligent person.

By the time Sarah and her husband arrived in Canaan from Mesopotamia with their nephew Lot, Sarah had already reached the age of 65, a decade younger than her husband. At first the family settled near Shechem, then in Bethel, and they moved from there gradually south into the Negev in search of grazing land for their flocks of animals. It was a relatively short distance to Egypt where they found sustenance during a famine. After some misunderstandings with the king of Egypt they were obliged to return to Canaan where conditions had improved. The family retraced their steps settling in the Negev near Kadesh, the territory of the well-known King Abimelech with whom there were also some serious misunderstandings. Eventually, they returned to Hebron.

Having lost all hope of bearing a son, Sarah offered her Egyptian maid, Hagar, to her husband in order that he, at least, would have children. In due course, a son, named Ishmael, was born from this union. About thirteen years later celestial visitors informed Sarah that she herself would give birth the following year. At the age of 90 Sarah gave birth to Isaac, her first and only child.

A conflict ensued resulting in the departure of Hagar and Ishmael from the family compound. Afterwards, Abraham, Sarah and Isaac prospered. The next 37 years were by all accounts the happiest of Sarah's life. She never lived to see her son marry, but Sarah believed – at least until the unfortunate rumors about his death – that Isaac would succeed Abraham as patriarch in partnership with the Almighty.

The importance of Sarah has been overshadowed by her husband's fame and his well-known close relationship with the Almighty. Fulfilling three roles, namely, protecting and advising Abraham, giving birth to and raising Isaac, and obeying God's will transformed this woman into a matriarch, a mother with power in the full sense of the word.

Sarah protected and advised Abraham, and on one occasion she also challenged his authority. In Egypt and in Abimelech's kingdom she acceded to Abraham's request that she pretend not to be his wife thus making her available as a potential wife to others and saving Abraham from assassination. She also understood that Abraham needed an heir to carry out God's promise that he would found a people, and for that reason she insisted he cohabit with Hagar. But, when Hagar, pregnant with Abraham's child, subsequently threatened Sarah's position as matriarch, Sarah vigorously defended her own preeminence. Abraham hesitated to punish Hagar, and then Sarah accused him of responsibility for Hagar's pretensions which were a corruption of God's will. Sarah said: "May the Lord decide between you and me." (Gen

16:5) This statement is crucial in understanding Sarah. In it she implied that she knew God's will better than Abraham did and that she was prepared to challenge her husband's leadership and authority. (It is curious that famous Biblical commentators such as Rashi, Ramban and Ibn Ezra ignore Sarah's provocative statement.)

After Sarah's son Isaac was born she raised him to succeed his father. God confirmed to Abraham that Isaac would succeed him, and there was no place in Abraham's camp for Ishmael and Hagar. Sarah's influence over Abraham continued even during the 38 years between her death and Abraham's death. Sometime after burying Sarah in Hebron Abraham married Ketura who bore six sons, but Abraham sent them away so that none would challenge Isaac. (Gen 25:6)

Sarah's influence depended on her special relationship with the Almighty. We read that "The Lord took note of her." (Gen 21:1). In the Torah whenever God "remembers" or "takes note of" we know there will be some momentous change. God remembered No-ach (Gen 8:1), and then the flood waters subsided. God "took note" (*pakad et Sarah*), and the root of the verb is *pei-kaf -dalet* whose different meanings shed light on the importance of taking note in this context. According to Midrash *Pesikta Rabbati*, (Midrash is commentary on holy texts based on analysis and legend) words formed on this root "always refer to God's providence." (*Pesikta,* Piska 42:9) In other words, God did more than suddenly remember Sarah. He cared for Sarah's welfare as her guardian.

The obituary of Sarah ends in the following way: In addition to her devoted husband, survivors include her son Isaac and about 300 generations of descendants "as numerous as the stars of the heaven and the sands of the seashore...." (Gen 22:17) This is what God promised to Abraham, but I think it is also applicable to Sarah. (See Gen 17:16)

## Sarah's importance

The obituary clearly explains the importance of Sarah. God selected Abraham for a covenantal relationship, but both Abraham and Sarah were tested for 30 years. If Sarah had failed the expectations of God, the consequences would have been as serious as if Abraham had failed the expectations of God.

According to *Pesikta Rabbati,* the angels warned God that if Sarah did not have a child after so many years of waiting, no one would ever believe God's promises, and "the Torah would have been deemed a fake." (*Pesikta,* Piska 42, Summary) Sarah's pregnancy is the sign that God has decided to proceed with His plan. The birth of Isaac begins the succession process and is the beginning of the Jewish people and its particular relationship with the Almighty. For this reason the Torah reading for Rosh Hashanah, the new year, is not *B'reishit* which is the beginning of the whole world and humankind; it is, rather, Genesis 21:1-2: "The Lord took note of Sarah as He had promised, and the Lord did for Sarah as He had spoken. Sarah conceived and bore a son to Abraham."

On March 3ʳᵈ 1990 the Committee of Jewish Law and Standards of the Rabbinical Assembly, the association of Conservative rabbis, adopted by a plurality the responsum advising the inclusion of the matriarchs' names (Sarah, Rebekah, Rachel and Leah) in the *Avot* or beginning blessing of the central prayer of every prayer service, the *Amidah*. (Rembaum) As a result, the Conservative or Masorti prayer book, *Siddur Sim Shalom,* published by the same Rabbinical Assembly, includes the matriarchs in an alternative version of the Amidah. Although inclusion is normative in Reform Judaism's prayer books, it is not quite normative in Conservative or Masorti books.

The Committee on Jewish Law and Standards reasoned that the four women beginning with Sarah "function as significant factors in the unfolding of the covenant between God and the Israelite nation." The words "significant factors" are rather weak. The rabbis departed from the Torah in their conclusion. They used sociological reasoning saying that because of the increased role of women in modern society, "the Amidah [should] be modified so that it can speak to all members of our congregations, male and female alike." This is superfluous, in my opinion.

The text of the Torah gives enough reason for inclusion of the four women. As I have written in this chapter, Sarah is her husband's active partner and God's loyal servant. She is a person with foresight and great strength which she uses unselfishly on behalf of God and her family. As her descendants, the Jews of today are the beneficiaries of her actions. By including Sarah in prayers alongside Abraham Jews pay tribute to this noble and powerful woman.

# 6

## *Tol'dot*

✦

### *(Genesis 25:19-28:9)*

The opening words of this Parashah are misleading, in my opinion. The Hebrew is *V'eileh tol'dot Yitzchak ben Avraham* or "This is the story [*tol'dot*] of Isaac, son of Abraham." (Gen 25:19) Why misleading? Because the story is about Rebekah, Isaac's wife. What is Rebekah's role?

In this Parashah Rebekah becomes pregnant with twins. She is perplexed because the Lord has told her directly and clearly that although each child will be the ancestor of a great people, "the older shall serve the younger." (Gen 25:23) Isaac is totally ignorant about God's message. Only Rebekah knows the will of God.

Esau is born shortly before Jacob making him the firstborn; Jacob is junior to Esau. But, God wants Jacob to succeed their father Isaac as patriarch. In the course of this Parashah Jacob tricks Esau out of property rights as firstborn. (Traditionally, the firstborn son receives more property after the death of the father.) Time passes. The family moves from place to place where they have various types of relationships with the local Canaanites.

Esau and Jacob reach the age of about 40. Isaac is probably about 100 years old; he senses the need to pass the mantle of leadership to Esau. (Remember that only Rebekah knows that God wishes that Jacob, not Esau, assume the mantle.) Rebekah arranges a complicated ruse so that Jacob receives Isaac's blessing which automatically makes his Isaac's successor. Isaac unknowingly blesses Jacob: "Let peoples serve you. Be master over your brothers.... Cursed be they who curse you, Blessed they who bless you." (Gen 27:29)

Isaac, who has poor eyesight, thinks he has blessed Esau. When he realizes his mistake, he tells Esau that he cannot rescind the blessing. Esau is enraged as he has lost both the property of his birthright and the blessing due to him. He might kill Jacob.

Rebekah hears about Esau's reaction, and she cannot be surprised that Esau might wish to kill his brother. She, therefore, seizes the initiative once again by convincing Isaac to send Jacob back to the family's homeland, Mesopotamia, in search of a wife.

Rebekah's actions are as significant in Jewish history as are the actions of Sarah and later the actions of Jacob's wives, Rachel and Leah. All four women understand God's will. Leah, her father and sister Rachel trick Jacob into marrying Leah who – despite Jacob's anger at the deception and lack of love for Leah –will bear six sons as well as the family's only daughter, Dinah. Rachel steals her father's idols thus protecting Jacob.

Study of the roles of Rebekah as well as Rachel and Leah provides the evidence that these three women, alongside Sarah, deserve to be honored in prayers. One could make a case that the two female servants, Bilhah and Zilpah, who bore two sons each to Jacob, should also be included.( See Weinstein, "Why Exclude…") One scholar says that when Jews say at the beginning of the *Amidah* prayer "Abraham's God, Isaac's God and Jacob's God" they are reflecting "a rabbinic theological doctrine known as 'merits of the ancestors'…according to which the righteous actions of the patriarchs continue on to benefit their descendants." (Hoffman citing Brettler, p.60)

If we need another reason to honor all seven ancestors, here it is: The word "Israel" itself, according to Rabbi Dr.Yosef Green (in a discussion at Moreshet Yisrael synagogue in Jerusalem) represents the unity of the matriarchs with the patriarchs. "Israel" or, more correctly, "Yisrael," is spelled with the first letters of all their names: *yad-sin-reish-alef-lamed.* *Yad* stands for Jacob (Yaakov in Hebrew); *sin* for Sarah; *reish* for Rebekah and Rachel; *alef* for Abraham; and *lamed* for Leah. In short, without the matriarchs there can be no Israel/Yisrael.

# 7

## *Va-yetzei*

♦

## *(Genesis 28:10-32:3)*

After Jacob has deceived his brother and father he "left [*va-yetzei*] Beer-Sheva" and went east to the ancestral homeland in Mesopotamia. On the way he has an encounter with the Almighty Who renews the promises of a Covenant previously made to Abraham.

Jacob arrives in the territory of his uncle Laban where he falls in love with Laban's younger daughter Rachel; he agrees to work for Laban for seven years in return for marriage with Rachel. Jacob fulfils the contract, but Laban secretly exchanges his older daughter Leah for Rachel on the wedding night. The next morning Laban explains to a very angry Jacob that he had to marry off his elder daughter first as that is the custom. Jacob is dejected but agrees to work another seven years for Rachel. What can one say about Leah? Her story seems sad, but it is not.

Our first glimpse of Leah in the Torah is of an unattractive person. The text literally says that she "had weak eyes." Rachel, however, is described as "shapely and beautiful." (Gen 29:17)

Leah has to struggle to get Jacob's attention.

After Jacob's two marriages Rachel remains barren. If Jacob is going to have children, as God said he must, he must spend time with Leah and then with the Bilhah, the servant Rachel has offered him as well as with Zilpah, the servant Leah has offered him. Leah is the first to give birth; her baby is named Reuben, and then she has six more children: Simeon, Levi, Judah, Issachar, Zebulun, and the daughter, Dina.

After each birth Leah thinks Jacob might begin to love her. When her third son, Levi, is born, she says, for example: "This time my husband will become attached to me, for I have borne him three sons." (Gen 29:34) By the time her fourth son, Judah, is born she understands that God has chosen her to play a key role in the founding of the Israelite people. She says: "I will praise the Lord" (Gen 29:35) According to the Talmud, Leah is the first person in the Bible explicitly to praise the Lord. (Gen. 29:35, Berakhot 7b) Her will to have children for Jacob is so strong that the text tells us: "God heeded Leah, and she conceived and bore him a fifth son." (Gen 30:17)

Finally, Rachel gives birth to a son named Joseph. Leah instinctively knows Jacob will favor Joseph over her sons and daughter, but she accepts it. Tragically, Rachel dies giving birth to her second son, Benjamin, and the family buries her near Bethlehem on the road back to Canaan. Of the two sisters only Leah reaches the Promised Land with Jacob and the children. After some time she also dies, and Jacob buries her with his parents and grandparents in the cave of Machpelah at Hebron.

Jacob resented Leah until the last days of his life. On his deathbed, however, the Torah tells us that he "bowed to the head of the bed." (Gen 47:31) The rabbis, explain that he was bowing to the memory of Leah. He realized that she is "the one who had borne him more than half of all his children." (Munk on Gen 29:30, p. 398) Leah's sons include Levi and Judah, direct ancestors of the contemporary Jewish population. Jacob instructed his sons to bury him in the family grave in Hebron which means that he would rest forever with Leah.

Leah's story is one of triumph, not defeat or sadness. She understood God's plan, and she understood her role in the history of Israel. She was a woman of great strength and forbearance – a true matriarch – and she should be honored as such.

# 8

# *Va-yishlach*

✦

## *(Genesis 32:4-36:43)*

As Jacob proceeds with his family back to his parents' home after a 20-year absence he learns he will probably meet Esau, his estranged brother. Esau is coming toward him with 400 men, and he fears that Esau may still have a grudge against him for stealing his birthright and blessing. Jacob wisely sends Esau a friendly message. The word for "sent" is *va-yishlach*, the name of the Parashah.

The night before the meeting between the two brothers Jacob struggles with an unnamed being – probably an angel - who blesses him and changes his name from Jacob to Israel. As a result Jacob has more confidence in himself. The reunion with Esau goes well, but Jacob wisely declines Esau's offer to accompany him home.

Jacob and his family settle for the time being in the Canaanite town of Shechem at least until their daughter and sister Dinah is abducted and abused by the man named Shechem, son of the local chief. Dinah's brothers take their revenge by massacring the men of the town. Fearful of the effects of this massacre on relations with other Canaanites, Jacob and his family leave that place. Rachel dies giving birth to Benjamin, and by the time Jacob reaches his parents' home his mother has already died, and Isaac will soon breathe his last. Esau returns to help Jacob bury their father. The Parashah ends with a detailed description of Esau's many descendants. (Gen 36:1-43)

As we read the names in this genealogy we understand that Jacob had good reason to be afraid of meeting Esau. History will show that the Edomites and most particularly the Amalekites who descend from Esau will be enemies of Jacob's descendants, the Israelites and the Jews. Amalekites will gratuitously attack the Israelites shortly after they depart from Egypt. Haman will attempt to destroy the Jewish community in Persia. The rabbis identified the Romans as descendants of Esau. My question is: Is Esau's desire for revenge justified?

The Torah forewarns us that Esau will try to take his revenge; when he realized Jacob had stolen their father's blessing: he "wept aloud" (Gen 27:38) and "harbored a grudge against Jacob…" (Gen 27:41) Isaac tries to comfort Esau by telling him that he will be prosperous and free. (Gen 27:39-40) The rabbis say that Isaac asked God for mercy for Esau, but God replies "He is wicked." (Megilah, 6a) Other references in the Talmud are also harsh. "The wicked man living between two righteous men and not learning from their ways was Esau." (Yoma, 38b). Was Esau innately evil? Isn't it logical to assume that Esau would never have been angry if he had known that God had chosen Jacob to succeed their father? It would not have made any difference, in my opinion.

The hint about Esau's innate potential for wickedness prior to Jacob's trick on him is that he marries a Hittite woman against his parents' will (Gen 26:34-35), and Rashi explains that before this marriage he was similar to Shechem in that he "enticed women from their husbands and ill-treated them…." (Rashi on Gen 26:34) The Torah and commentators are teaching us that Esau acts according to his own passions, and his descendants attack Israel by their own choices. Thus, the answer to my question is that the hostility to Jacob and thus to Israel cannot be justified as revenge for Jacob's deception.

There is a saying that revenge is a dish best eaten cold, but in this case the dish is really too cold to be justified or believed. Another principle is at stake here to explain the antagonism of Esau's descendants, and the Torah is preparing us to understand it: those who reject God's commandments will always hate the people God has chosen to represent and carry out those commandments. We pray that despite the antagonism Israel will always stand for the principles and laws given to its ancestors.

# 9

## *Va-yeishev*

✦

## *(Genesis 37:1-40:23)*

Everyone has heard and used the phrase "brotherly love." Philadelphia, Pennsylvania calls itself "The City of Brotherly Love." Unfortunately, this Parashah reminds us of "brotherly hate." After Jacob settled [*va-yeishev*, the name of the Parashah] in the Land of Canaan there is conflict among his sons, more specifically between Joseph and everyone else. Joseph's 11 brothers are jealous of him; they hate him enough to want to kill him and then as an alternative to sell him into slavery. A caravan takes him to Egypt.

There are so many other examples of brotherly hate in the Bible that one begins to wonder if that is the norm. The other cases that come to mind are Cain's murder of Abel, Esau's long grudge against Jacob, the expulsion of Ishmael into the harsh desert where he and his mother might have died. In the days of the United Kingdom one of Solomon's brothers tries to steal the throne from him even though David, their father, has made it clear who his successor is to be. Absalom kills his brother Amron. What are we to make of these intense antagonistic feelings against one's kith and kin?

At the very least these examples show us that the people in our Hebrew Bible are human beings with strengths and deficiencies. They are neither all saints nor all sinners; they love, they hate, they fight, they make peace, they weep, they laugh. A few are dishonest and violent, and many do their best for others. They are obedient. And sometimes they betray the One and Only God. In short, they show us the full gamut of human characteristics and emotions. They live in the distant past, but don't they sometimes make us think of people in our own families or even remind us of ourselves? At the very least, they prove once again that we can choose our friends, but we cannot choose our relatives.

Secondly, their hate proves the power of the human will. The examples of brotherly enmity are examples of choice. Jacob unwisely chooses to favor

Joseph over his brothers. No one told him to do this. Joseph unwisely chooses to boast about his sense of superiority thereby offending his siblings. The brothers choose to rid themselves of Joseph by killing him or by disposing of him with traders.

Thirdly, these examples of hate remind us, by contrast, of the examples of love among siblings elsewhere in the texts. The eleven sons of Jacob reunite themselves with Joseph in Egypt. They become once again one family, the ancestors of a united nation. Think of Moses, Aaron and Miriam. Miriam helps save the baby Moses' life at great risk to herself; she and Aaron stand by their younger brother Moses during the most momentous chapters in Jewish history. Who can forget the love and solidarity of the five sons of Mattathias, the Hasmonean who led the revolt against the Greek Seleucids in the second century BCE? The historian Josephus writes that Mattathias, as he lay dying, orders his sons to love one another and to work together: "I exhort you especially to agree one with another, and in what excellency any one of you exceeds another, to yield to him so far, and by that means to reap the advantage of everyone's own virtues." (*The Works of Josephus*, "Antiquities," 12:6:3, p.283) Their unity and commitment to God and the Jewish people gave them the strength to defeat a powerful foe and to re-establish a Jewish state in the Land of Israel.

There is no denying tensions, antagonisms and even hate among the members of the family of Israel in the past and today. Altering one old aphorism, we can say: to hate is human, to love is divine, but if we strive with all our will and all our might to love all our brothers and sisters, we humans can approach closer to the Almighty.

# 10

# *Mi-Ketz*

✦

## *(Genesis 41:1-44:17)*

In the previous Parashah Joseph correctly interprets the dreams of two prison inmates one of whom is the king's cupbearer. The cupbearer is released and goes back to work for the king again, but he forgets to tell the king about Joseph as he had promised Joseph. "After two years time [*va-yechi mi-ketz shnatayim*] the king has dreams that no one can interpret. Suddenly the cupbearer remembers Joseph's skill at interpretation, and, therefore, Joseph is brought before the sovereign. He interprets the dreams by explaining that God is telling the king there will be seven years of plenty and seven years of famine. He advises the king to appoint a person to oversee the preparations of food reserves. The king immediately appoints Joseph giving him an Egyptian name; he also arranges for Joseph to marry the daughter of a priest.

As predicted, the seven years of plenty end, and the years of famine begin. Only Egypt has enough food, even enough for its neighbors. Word about the food reserves in Egypt spreads to neighboring peoples.

Jacob hears about Egypt and sends two missions under the leadership of Judah to purchase food from the king's officials. The sons of Jacob arrive and appear before Joseph who recognizes them. They obtain the food but only after Joseph exacts a little revenge: he accuses them of being spies, and then he accuses Benjamin, who has come on the second mission, of being a thief.

Despite the central importance of Joseph, Judah emerges as the key player in this dangerous situation. Judah was originally angry and jealous of Joseph; he is in large part responsible for selling Joseph into slavery and for causing grief to their father Jacob.

What Judah did to Joseph is certainly evil and sinful, but could one argue that if Joseph had not gone to Egypt and had not been there to interpret the king's dreams, many people, including Jacob and his family, would have died from the famine. Does the end – meaning food – justify the means –

kidnapping and sending Joseph to Egypt? Put another way, is Judah absolved from guilt because his evil actions – selling his brother and hurting his father – have a good outcome? No. Judah's guilty actions do not evaporate because of other's people's actions. The Parashah teaches us that Judah is responsible for his deeds; only Judah can repair the damage he has caused. And, he does.

Maimonides says that the highest form of repentance is when we are put in the same situation in which we committed a sin, but we choose a different path the second time. How does this apply to Judah? Both Joseph and Benjamin are the preferred sons of Jacob because their mother was Jacob's beloved Rachel. When the vizier of Egypt, namely Joseph who is not recognized by his brothers, accuses Benjamin of theft and says Benjamin must become his slave, Judah, son of Leah, the wife whom Jacob despises, and the other brothers could have agreed thereby ridding themselves of the last son of Rachel. Instead of doing that, Judah, speaking on behalf of his brothers and himself, asserts collective responsibility and guilt. (Gen 44:16) At the beginning of the next Parashah Judah goes one step further, surprising everyone. He offers himself as a slave to Joseph so that Benjamin can go free. (Gen 44:33)

Judah never explicitly apologizes to Joseph or to their father Jacob for having abandoned and condemned Joseph to slavery. It is not necessary because his action in offering himself as a slave is the highest form of repentance. As great as Joseph is, Judah gives the world the most important lesson, namely, the meaning of repentance.

# 11

## *Va-yiggash*

✦

## *(Genesis 44:18-47:27)*

Joseph is a central personage in many chapters of the Book of Genesis. Let us suppose that archaeologists just found an autobiography of this man. What would Joseph have said about himself? Does he have a message? Let me review this "book."

The autobiography would have eight chapters. Joseph, one of the Bible's great men of action, knew that the number eight symbolizes Israelite acceptance of partnership with God – male circumcision eight days after birth is one example. The first of these eight chapters is a succinct chronology of his life. The seven succeeding chapters are organized thematically.

## 1. Chronology

Joseph reminds us that he was the 11th son of Jacob and the first child of Rachel. At the age of six or seven while the family was returning to the Land of Canaan Joseph's mother died near Bethlehem while giving birth to Joseph's younger brother Benjamin. After burying Rachel the family continued south to Hebron where Joseph met his grandfather, Isaac, shortly before the latter died.

As a boy and then as an adolescent Joseph tended the animals belonging to his father. At the age of 17 he was sold into slavery by his brothers who were jealous about their father's obvious favoritism. Employed by Potiphar, a high ranking Egyptian official, for the next eight years or so, he was thrown into prison on charges he molested his employer's wife. At the age of about 28 he began interpreting dreams for fellow prisoners.

At the age of 30 he was released from captivity and for fourteen years as prime minister he organized the whole of Egyptian society to save it from famine. He was reunited with his family. His father and brothers moved to

Egypt and lived under his protection. Joseph lived in comfort and happiness in Egypt while all the children of Jacob/Israel also thrived.

(We know from the Torah that he died at the age of 110.)

## 2. Faith in God

For about two decades Joseph had no contact with his family and the Promised Land. He immersed himself in Egyptian culture as he had to. How was he able to keep his faith in the one God? Giving credit to his parents is completely plausible.

Role of Jacob: Jacob obviously loved Rachel and Joseph and then Benjamin more than he loved anyone else; he had to tell the three of them about his past, his dreams, and the promises made by God. Furthermore, Joseph could never be far from his father in his own mind because of their close physical resemblance. We know he almost succumbed to the charms of Potiphar's wife. At the critical moment he glanced at a window of her bedroom and saw his father's face staring at him. His father warned him that he would be excluded from the family if he followed his physical desires. (Rashi on Genesis 39:11, based on Sotah 36b) At that point he fled from the Egyptian woman's embrace.

Because of Rachel: Joseph had to know that Rachel's barrenness, like that of his great grandmother Sarah, had a purpose. After making these women wait God made clear that they would give birth because of God's decision. He expected the sons of Sarah and Rachel, meaning Isaac and Joseph, to serve Him in special ways. Furthermore, Rachel showed Joseph the dangers and uselessness of idolatry when she stole her father Laban's idols as the family was departing from Laban's camp. It is possible the young Joseph was her accomplice. Joseph must have felt her contempt for her father's idols. *Zohar*, a central text in Kabbalah, Jewish mysticism, confirms her disdain for idols and adds that she hoped "to wean her father from idolatry." (*Zohar* I:164b)

Joseph's faith in God strengthened as he reflected on what his parents taught him. By the time he met the mighty king of Egypt he dared to tell the monarch that the God of Jacob would save Egypt. (Gen 41:25-33)

## 3. Communication with God

We can only infer communication between God and Joseph. Joseph thought he received some messages indirectly from the Almighty. According to Rabbi Simeon, as quoted in the *Zohar* "God reveals His will to prophets; if not to prophets, then to sages, in the absence of sages, then in dreams…." (*Zohar*

I:183a) Only when he is in Egypt does he realize that the dreams and the ability to interpret them are gifts from the Almighty.

Joseph also understands the meaning of a small incident while he was looking for his brothers that fateful day when they seized and sold him to a caravan. A man appeared out of nowhere to give him the directions he needed to find his brothers who had preceded him into the pasture. This man, sent by God, was the angel Gabriel, according to Rashi. (Rashi on Genesis 37:15)

Joseph eventually comprehends the Divine plan for saving the family of Israel. He reassures his brothers after they are reunited that he bears no grudge: "although you intended me harm, God intended it for good, so as to bring about the present result – the survival of many people." (Gen 50:20)

## 4. Identity

This is the longest chapter because of the importance of the subject then and now. Our identity is shaped by who we are and who we are not. Joseph learned the negative side – who he was not - from his uncle Esau. He learned the positive side – who he was - from his brothers.

a.  Esau and his descendants, the Edomites and the Amalekites, are the quintessential enemy. They wish to destroy Israel completely. When Jacob and Esau meet on the road after 20 years of separation, Jacob fears conflict. He seems to sense that in the future Joseph and his descendants would have a special role in the wars with the Edomites. (This idea is confirmed by the prophet Obadiah: "The house of Jacob shall be fire, and the house of Joseph flame, while the house of Esau shall be straw. They shall burn it and devour it. And no survivor shall be left of the House of Esau, for the Lord has spoken." (Obadiah, 1:18)

    In this Parashah, however, Joseph is still a small child who must be protected. So, Jacob puts Joseph and his pregnant mother behind everyone else, the furthest away from Esau. Esau wants a closer look at the whole family, and as he approaches Rachel, Joseph blocks Esau's view. He seems ready to fight his uncle. (*Midrash Rabbah Genesis,* on Genesis 33:7)

b.  Joseph's brothers are both his best friends and his enemies. Before Joseph is sold into slavery the brothers define themselves according to who their mothers are. Joseph sees Simeon and Levi attack and murder the men of Shechem because the latter abducted their sister, Dinah. (The three of them, Dinah, Simeon and Levi, are children of Leah.) Rebuked by their father after the carnage, they are unrepentant, even proud of defending family honor. (Gen 34:31)

A young Joseph is arrogant toward his brothers, but with maturity and exile in Egypt comes understanding of their strengths and weaknesses. When he meets them more than 20 years later in Egypt, he is not sure if they have changed and advises them: "Do not be quarrelsome...." (Gen 45:24) Then he tests them by threatening to keep Benjamin in Egypt. When Judah, son of Leah, offers himself in place of Benjamin, son of Rachel, Joseph sees proof of a new solidarity.

Joseph weeps tears of joy and love because they have changed. They have evolved into one family saying: "We are all of us sons of the same man...." (Gen 42:11) They are now true Sons of Israel, Israelites. Further to preserve Israelite identity and to ensure their prosperity, Joseph settles them together in a fertile region of Egypt. He tells his family that their descendants will return together to Canaan, and he, Joseph, will be with them: "When God has taken note of you, you shall carry up my bones from here." (Gen 50:25)

## 5. Skills

Joseph gained the confidence of his Egyptian master, Potiphar, and became the manager "of his household and all that he owned...." (Gen 39:5) Joseph obviously learned the Egyptian language and moved easily in Egyptian society. He even learned things in prison where "[t]he chief jailer put in Joseph's charge all the prisoners... and he was the one to carry out everything that was done there." (Gen 39:22) The king married him to an Egyptian woman, and they had two sons. All these experiences were preparing him to save Egypt and Israel

## 6. Vizier or Prime Minister of Egypt

Joseph quickly realizes that because of its geography and dependence on the Nile River, Egypt needs to control very carefully the use of water and unify a diverse population through a highly centralized decision-making system. His policies succeed, and Egypt has the political system and economy it needs to survive and thrive.

## 7. Future

Joseph's predictions: Here Joseph makes a mistake. He seems to think he will succeed his father, but we cannot fault him for thinking he would become the fourth patriarch. Jacob calls Joseph "the elect of his brothers." (Gen 49:26), but Joseph does not seem to understand Jacob's praise of his older brother

Judah that we read in the next Parashah: "The scepter shall not depart from Judah. Nor the ruler's staff from between his feet." (Gen 49:10) Joseph cannot predict that Judah's descendants, not his own descendants, will rule over all of Israel and that Israelites will become Judahites or Jews, no matter which brother was their ancestor.

## 8. Power

The first secular-type leader in Jewish history is Joseph, so one should pay particular attention to what he says and does. Being close to power in Potiphar's household gives Joseph many advantages, but at the same time he is vulnerable to attack as non-Egyptian. When Potiphar's wife became angry with him after he spurned her advances, she "called out to her servants.... 'Look, he [meaning Potiphar, her husband] had to bring us a Hebrew to dally with us.'" (Gen 39:14) In other words, being close to power has its risks for Jews, but being far from power has more risks. For example, had Esther not been queen of Persia, Haman would have succeeded in destroying the Jews there.

In the Book of *Sh'mot* or Exodus we read "A new king arose over Egypt who did not know Joseph...." (Ex 1:8) meaning there were no Israelites with power and influence. Without opposition the Egyptian leaders could plot to enslave the descendants of Joseph and his brothers.

Maintain a close relationship with secular powers is Joseph's message in the concluding chapter of his book. Someone else put it more bluntly in a book from the 20th century. Yaakov Bok in Bernard Malamud's novel *The Fixer* is falsely accused of murdering a Russian Christian child for alleged Jewish ritual purposes. This weak man fights the Tsarist state desperately and at first blindly and terribly alone, but he becomes a hero to all revolutionaries in spite of himself. After a lifetime of avoiding politics and Jewish identity and God he realizes "there is no such thing as an unpolitical man, especially a Jew. You can't be one without the other, that's clear enough. You can't sit still and see yourself destroyed." (Malamud, p. 335) Joseph would agree.

Archaeologists continue their work in Israel, and who knows what they will discover next buried in the sand and the earth? Certainly artifacts, documents, epigraphs along with commentaries and studies help us understand the historical past and God's will. Like a book about Joseph or by Joseph, they are interesting and important, but we don't really need them. We can understand the essential messages of the Torah and the Talmud from these holy texts and the analysis of our sages.

# 12

## *Va-y'chi*

✦

### *(Genesis 47:28-50:26)*

How did Israelites become Jews? According to Parashat *Va-y'chi,* Israelites might have become Josephites. In this reading Jacob predicts that Judah will be powerful, but he gives his all-important blessing to Joseph and to Joseph's two sons, Ephraim and Manasseh. According to the text, Jacob "blessed Joseph saying, 'The God in whose ways my fathers Abraham and Isaac walked. Bless the lads. In them may my name be recalled. And the names of my fathers Abraham and Isaac. And may they be teeming multitudes upon the earth." (Gen 48:15-16)

Therefore, it seems that Jacob chose Joseph and then Joseph's son Ephraim to succeed him as the fourth and fifth patriarchs. The first book of Chronicles explains: "[Reuben] was the firstborn, but... his birthright was given to the sons of Joseph... [and] though Judah became more powerful than his brothers...yet the birthright belonged to Joseph." (I Chron 5:1-2) Rabbi Ibn Ezra says Jacob's blessing means that "All of Israel will be called Ephraim and Joseph." (Ibn Ezra on Gen 48:16)

In fact, the northern kingdom of Israel was often referred to as Josephite or Ephraimite territory. Its population significantly outnumbered the population of the southern kingdom of Judah. King David's census in the 11th century BCE found 800,000 men of military age in Israel compared with 500,000 men of military age in Judah. (II Samuel, 24:9) After the two kingdoms split apart in about 925 BCE Jeroboam, an Ephraimite, ruled in the north. Northern independence did not last long, however.

Assyria completed its conquest and destruction of the northern kingdom of Israel by 721 BCE; they took the majority of Ephraimite and other tribal elites into exile where they merged into other communities. Some Ephraimites, along with other northerners, must have escaped, however, into Judahite territory (Isserlin p. 88) where Judahites and Levites were living along with Benjaminites.

Subsequently, Judahite identity began to change from tribal exclusivity to residential inclusivity. All Israelites living in the territory of Judah began to call themselves Judeans. The Hasmonean kings and priests ruling a newly independent Judea in the 2nd century BCE were descendants of Levi, not Judah, but inscriptions on the coins show that they identified their kingdom as "Jewish." By then, a Jew, Judahite, Judean or Yehudi was defined as any descendant of Judah and/or any Israelite living in the geographical area of Judah, according to Shaye J. D. Cohen (Cohen, p. 71).

So, the answer to the question "How did Israelites become Jews" is that the remnant of the descendants of Jacob or Israel who survived the conquests and exiles gradually became Jews by a process of absorption into Judah's territory and community.

A more interesting question is not "how" but "why" did Israelites become Jewish? In the Parashah Jacob chose Joseph and Ephraim as his successors, but it seems that God made a different choice, namely, the House of Judah as partners in the Covenant. Why did God choose Judah? What were Judah's personal qualities of character that proved to God that he was worthy? His biography should answer that question.

Judah is Leah's fourth son. Like his siblings Judah is jealous of Joseph, but he rejects the idea of killing Joseph. Judah convinces his brothers to sell him to a passing caravan. (Gen 37:26-27) After this deed is done, the *Zohar* says that the brothers are full of remorse and blame Judah. (*Zohar* I:186a) For that reason or because Judah cannot bear to face his father, he goes into self-imposed exile among the Canaanites. He is separated from his family for almost twenty years, slightly less time than Joseph is separated from the family. What does Judah do?

The Torah tells us that Judah wanders into the area controlled by Shuah. Judah is certainly depressed and lonely. According to Jewish legend, he drinks excessively and in a state of drunkenness is attracted to a woman who happens to be the daughter of the local king. Her father offers a considerable dowry to Judah, and he takes her as his wife. (Ginzburg, Vol. 2, p. 199) This woman, simply called Bat Shua or the daughter of Shua, gives birth to three sons and then dies. (Gen 38:1-5, 12) Many years later Judah's eldest son marries a woman called Tamar, but then he dies. Judah orders his second son to marry Tamar, but the young man refuses and dies. The third son is not offered as a substitute. Instead, Judah lets himself be seduced by her, his own daughter-in-law.

After falsely accusing Tamar of harlotry, Judah accepts Tamar, who is already pregnant, as his own wife. She gives birth to twins, and at that point

Judah decides to take his new family back to his father's compound arriving just in time to help Jacob and the rest of the family who are suffering through a famine. (Interestingly, although Jacob has grieved for the loss of Joseph, he does not seem to have worried much about the disappearance of Judah.)

The shortage of food forces Jacob to send his sons on a mission to Egypt where food is available. Judah takes the leadership of the group which includes all the surviving brothers except the youngest, Benjamin, who has taken Joseph's place as Jacob's favorite. In Egypt Judah meets with the Egyptian vizier or prime minister who, of course, is Joseph. Joseph recognizes his brothers, but we are supposed to believe that Judah does not recognize Joseph. (This is plausible because of the context and the undoubted Egyptian appearance of Joseph – clothing and hairstyle, for example.)

Because of the continuing famine, Judah must lead a second mission to Egypt. This time he brings Benjamin despite their father's misgivings. (Gen 43:3-15) Judah takes personal responsibility for Benjamin, and when Joseph falsely accuses Benjamin of theft, Judah, true to his word, volunteers to stay in Egypt as Joseph's slave in place of Benjamin.(Gen 44:33) Joseph then reveals who he is and immediately invites his father and brothers to live in Egypt. Judah returns home to Jacob and leads the whole family back to Egypt where they all live and flourish in the many years to come.

According to Jewish legend, as Judah is dying many years later he repents for his sins and predicts that his descendants will rule the tribes of Israel in the future. (Ginzburg, Vol.2, p. 200) He requests to be buried in Hebron where the three patriarchs and three matriarchs are buried.

What significant facts emerge about Judah from his biography that show the future importance of his tribe?

## 1. Self Awareness and Repentance

Judah recognizes his own weaknesses, and repents for his sins against Tamar and Joseph. In the case of Tamar, when he realizes he has falsely accused his daughter-in-law of harlotry, he admits his error (Gen 38:26). According to Jewish legend Judah swears never to drink again; he also becomes a vegetarian and a celibate. (Ginzburg, Vol. 2, p. 200) In the case of his sin against Joseph, he repents when he offers to serve as Joseph's slave. (Gen 44:33) Rabbi Ovadia Sforno wrote that Judah made this offer to become a slave so that, in Judah's words: "I will not have to remain a sinner against my father for the rest of my life." (In Munk, *Hachut*, Vol. 3 p. 809)

An understanding of guilt and repentance runs in the family of Judah. When King David, Judah's descendant, orders a census without God's permission, God punishes the people as a whole with a plague. David accepts the blame: "It is I who offended, I who did wrong…. Let Your hand be against me and my father's house." (II Samuel 24:17) David offers sacrifices to the Lord to expiate his crime, and the plague ceases.

## 2. Leadership

Judah emerges as leader of the sons of Israel when he suggests selling Joseph instead of killing him. He heads the two missions to Egypt for food.

Judah's descendants also accept the role and duties of leadership. When Moses takes the Israelites to the edge of the Sea of Reeds, the Judahites walk into the water first, thereby showing their faith in God. (*Zohar* I:237a) According to the Book of Judges (1:1-2) after the death of Joshua, the Ephraimite who became leader after Moses, the Lord explicitly assigns leadership to the tribe of Judah: "and the Lord said, 'Judah shall go up, behold I have delivered the land into his hand.'" King David believed that "the Lord God of Israel…has chosen Judah to be the ruler, and out of the house of Judah, the house of my father, and among the sons of my father He took pleasure in me to make me king over all Israel." (I Chron 28:4)

## 3. Faith in God and the new Covenant

Based on "The Letter to the Hebrews," Christians have believed that the Covenant between God and Abraham, Isaac and Jacob would be replaced by another covenant mediated by Jesus. (8:13, 12:24) This view fails to consider that God has already promised a renewal of the Covenant with the 12 tribes, the descendants of the three patriarchs.

The prophet Jeremiah explained that the Lord said He would "make a new covenant with the House of Israel and the House of Judah. It will not be like the Covenant I made with their fathers, when I took them by the hand to lead them out of the land of Egypt, a covenant which they broke, though I was lord over them – declares the Lord. But such is the covenant I will make with the House of Israel after these days – declares the Lord: I will put My Teaching into their inmost being and inscribe it upon their hearts. Then I will be their God, and they shall be My people." (Jer 31:31-33 in *Tanakh… The New JPS Translation*) This Covenant does not vitiate in any way the original Covenant made with Abraham, Isaac and Jacob. It is renewed and strengthened through Judah, their descendant.

The Almighty chose Isaac and Jacob as partners in the Covenant before they were born. They knew nothing and had done nothing to merit the Lord's confidence. Although Jeremiah says that God decided to make a new Covenant with all the tribes, this Covenant is primarily made with Judah, in my opinion, for two reasons: First, Judah's actions prove to God that God's teaching has become inscribed on Judah's heart, and second, as I have already explained, Judah comes to represent all the tribes of Israel.

We can see from the Torah that Judah grows intellectually and emotionally; he arrives at a better understanding than his brothers of his obligations to God, to his people and to the Promised Land. That is the answer to my question "Why did Israelites become Jews?" who are the literal and figurative descendants of Judah. Although initially Judah's motives are evil, he does save Joseph's life; later he repents for selling Joseph; he repents for his treatment of Tamar and marries her thereby redeeming her and himself. He arrives at an understanding of the need for unity and leads the family. He betrays but finally honors his father; he goes into self-imposed exile, but he returns home again bringing his children and his wife, who is, according to the Talmud, a proselyte (Sotah, 10a). It is worth noting that Joseph never returns to Canaan except to bury his father, and he and his Egyptian wife raise their own two sons in Egypt.

Both Jacob's deathbed prediction that Judah will be powerful and God's choice of Judah to be God's partner in the renewed Covenant are fully realized in the life and career of King David, a descendant of Judah. It is the prophet and judge Samuel who tells us that the rise of King David confirms God's choice of Judah as His partner in the Covenant. In the book of II Samuel we read that David "ordered the Judahites to be taught [The Song of the] Bow...." (II Sam 1:18) Ramban interprets this puzzling statement as follows: "for this is the bow which is seen in the cloud concerning which it is said: 'this is the token of the covenant.'" (Ramban on Deut 33:7) The "bow" is the rainbow God promised No-ach as the sign of the Covenant "that I have established between Me and all the flesh that is on earth." (Gen 9:17)

With this Covenant God redeems Judah and saves his descendants, the Jews, who are both a remnant and a union of all the tribes of Israel. When God chooses David, the Judahite, as king of all the twelve tribes, and when He promises that the Messiah will come from the House of David, God demonstrates His confidence that future generations of the Jewish people will obey the commandments. These Jews will do their best to understand obedience, sin, repentance and redemption.

Judah and then David transmit to Jews of modern times their renewed Covenant with the Almighty. Jews' daily choices and actions show whether or not God's teaching is in their innermost beings as it is supposed to be. If it is, Jews will maintain their partnership with God until the end of time.

# SH'MOT/EXODUS

# 13

## *Sh'mot*

✦

### *(Exodus 1:1 – 6:1)*

Four centuries have passed since Jacob and his family moved to Egypt. Many new generations of Israelites have been born; the text says they "multiplied and increased greatly" in Egypt. (Ex 1:7) Because so much time has passed, it is necessary to recall the names – the *sh'mot* – of the original Israelite settlers.

Knowing the names of the ancestors helps maintain identity, but it is mainly their separation from other Egyptians and the growth in their numbers that worry the king who takes drastic measures. The Israelites are enslaved, and the monarch orders the killing of every Israelite newborn male to limit population growth.

We all remember the story of one Levite family who saves their newborn son by placing him in a basket in the River Nile in the hope that some Egyptian family will rescue him and raise him. The daughter of the king himself finds him and decides to adopt him. Miriam, the baby's older sister, approaches the princess and offers her the services of an older woman as nurse and nanny. The princess does not seem to realize that the older woman, named Jochebed, is in fact the baby's biological mother. The woman takes the baby, and "[w]hen the child grew up, she [Jochebed] brought him to Pharaoh's daughter, who made him her son." (Ex 2:10)

Although Moses grows up in the lap of luxury, he does not forget his identity, and when he sees an Egyptian overseer abusing a Hebrew slave, he strikes and kills the Egyptian. Fearful of arrest, he flees to the nearby land of Midian where after sometime he marries and settles down.

God remembers His promises to Abraham, Isaac and Jacob and decides that this man, Moses, will lead their descendants out of Egypt and into the land He promised. Moses hears the voice of God for the first time from a burning bush and accepts very reluctantly the mission. His older brother,

Aaron, about whom we read for the first time, will help him. At the end of this Parashah the two brothers approach the king to request permission for the Israelites "to go, we pray, a distance of three days into the wilderness to sacrifice to the Lord our God, lest He strike us with pestilence or sword." (Ex 5:3) The incredulous king, who believes himself to be all- powerful and perhaps divine, dismisses them haughtily with words of disrespect for the Lord, and he makes life more difficult for the Israelite slaves.

This first encounter with the king of Egypt is the beginning of the great liberation story of Israel. Amazing miracles take place in the forty years from the exodus from Egypt to the death of Moses and the crossing into the Promised Land. In those years God renews the Covenant and issues specific commandments to Moses on Mt. Sinai. The basic institutions, holy days, rituals, and priesthood are decreed and organized for the Children of Israel.

The details of Moses' meetings with the king of Egypt, the plagues and liberation are recounted at the festival of Passover every year. Because discussion and raising questions are an expected part of the Passover *seder*, someone will succumb to the temptation to ask: "Did the exodus from Egypt really take place?" Or, "why is there no archaeological evidence for the movement of a large population from Egypt to Israel about 3500 years ago?" These questions are irrelevant.

What is important about the exodus story is that the historical accuracy of the story is not important. In other words, what can or cannot be proved by empirical data need not concern us. The founding narratives of all peoples, whether ancient Rome, Greece, Japan, the Bantu peoples of Africa, or India, are not important for the accuracy of their details. These epic stories or, as we can call them, founding narratives are important because of how they are applied, how they form the basis of contemporary beliefs and actions.

The applications of founding narratives to the contemporary world may be destructive or constructive. There is one destructive example from India: A great foundation narrative of Hinduism is the amazingly rich *Ramayana*. Central to this book is Ram, an important deity in the Hindu pantheon. Recently, some Hindus claimed they were sure Ram was born at Ayodhya in northern India. Over the exact place was a Muslim mosque, which although unused after Indian independence, was made by some politicians to serve as a symbol of Muslim conquest of India centuries ago.

Despite some government efforts to protect the site, a mob under the leadership of a political party intent on winning votes tore down the mosque in order to build a Hindu temple. They justified their action by appealing to the Hindu narrative and then inflamed other Hindus against Muslims. In the following years thousands, particularly Muslims, were killed. (There are many other Hindu narratives which are constructive and unifying, of course.)

The Exodus narrative beginning with God's call to Moses, has served to guide the Jewish people and other peoples as well throughout the millennia. To those millions of Jews living in exile the last words of Joseph to his brothers at the end of the Book of Genesis give hope: "God will surely take notice of you and bring you up from this land that He promised on oath to Abraham, to Isaac, and to Jacob." (Gen 50:24)

Sages, scholars and rabbis to the present day have studied and written and convinced hundreds of generations of Jews that this narrative is important and relevant to them no matter where they have lived, inside or outside the Land of Israel. The modern State of Israel represents at least a partial fulfillment of the founding narrative, and over the past few decades Jews prayed for the freedom of Russian and Ethiopian Jews to go there. The power of the narrative has strengthened the resolve of other peoples, particularly African Americans, to free themselves from slavery and oppression. It has moved Jews to pray for the Muslim victims in Darfur, Sudan.

So, the answer to any question about the founding narrative as described in the Book of Exodus and in the Passover book or *Haggadah*, (which means "telling" as in telling the story of the exodus), is simple: through these texts and the questions, they inspire Jews to renew their understanding of the transcendent truths of God's plan for the Jewish people and the world.

Perhaps the most important lesson from this effort is: "We study; therefore we are."

# 14

## *Va-era*

♦

## *(Exodus 6:2-9:35)*

What's in a name? For Jews a name is more than an identifier. All, including converts, have Hebrew names as well as secular names, and these names situate individuals within the Jewish people. Changes in the names of Abram to Abraham, Sarai to Sarah, Jacob to Israel, Hosea to Joshua mark a change in their lives. The sages of the Talmud believed that the name a parent chooses for a newborn has an effect on that person's future life. (Berakhot 7b, ftn 14) Theophoric names, which include a reference to God, reflect the parents' sense of their or their child's relationship with God. For example, Yonatan stands for "God gave this child; Ovadia means "servant of God"; Emmanuel means "God is with us."

We also associate naming with power and authority. God lets Adam name the other living things on the earth as a sign of human superiority to animals and plants. After the flood the people build a tower toward heaven saying "let us make a name for ourselves." (Gen 11:4) God understands their ambitions as a threat to His plans and thwarts their efforts by dispersing them to the four corners of the earth. God gives them different names and languages which weaken them.

Names are associated with loyalty and identity. In *Midrash Rabbah Leviticus* the rabbis say that one reason God redeems the Israelites from Egypt is that they did not change their names. (*Midrash Rabbah Leviticus*, XXXII:5) In Hebrew all Jews are identified as the son of or the daughter of so and so. If their fathers are descendants of priests or Levi, that fact is also part of the name. Among Arabs a woman or a man may be identified as the father (Abu…) or mother (Um…) of so and so.

My questions are as follows: 1. What are the names of God in Hebrew holy texts and prayers? 2. Why do Jews avoid saying one of these names in particular? 3. What are the risks from avoiding that one name or from using many different circumlocutions in place of that one name?

## 1. What are the names of God?

*El* is probably the oldest term for God in Semitic languages. (*Jewish Encyclopedia*)

Some others are *Elyon, El olam, Shaddai, Elohim, Ya, HaShem, HaMakom,* and *Adonai*. Rabbis of the Talmud employ *HaKodesh Barukh Hu* meaning "The Holy One Blessed be He." Kabbalists use *Ein Sof"* – "without end." In the *Sh'ma* and Aleinu prayers we call God "One."

Jews say most of these names without hesitation, but *Elohim* is pronounced as *Elokim* in ordinary discourse, and many substitute *HaShem* for *Adonai* to avoid disrespect. In writing both Hebrew and English some Jews leave out letters such as the "o" in the English word "God" writing G-d. The Dead Sea Scroll writers substituted dots for God or wrote the word in ancient or Paleohebrew. (Skehan pp. 15, 22)

The most important name, the ineffable name, is composed of the four letters *Yod-Hei-Vav-Hei*, called the Tetragrammaton in Greek. We could also call it the Quadrilateral or in Hebrew the *Shem Ben Arbah Otiyot*. This word, which we never pronounce according to its letters, appears over 6,800 times in the Torah. (*Jewish Encyclopedia,* p.2) Although the first substitution or circumlocution for it may have been *Elohim*, there is evidence that very early the Jews said *Adonai* in place of the original pronunciation of the Tetragrammaton. *Adonai* is now the word pronounced during prayers and the reading of the Torah in place of the four letters. It is plural in form, but the English is singular, Lord. The plural is a sign of great respect and reverence.

In Parashat *Va-era* God introduces Himself to Moses: *Ani Adonai* using the *Yod-Hei-Vav-Hei*: "I am the Lord. I appeared to Abraham, Isaac and Jacob as El Shaddai, but I did not make Myself known to them by My name, *Yod-Hei-Vav-Hei*." (Ex 6:2-3) Abraham does, in fact, know the Name (Cf. Gen 15:2), but there is a difference between Abraham's understanding of the Name and God's formal presentation of Himself to the Israelites in the present Parashah. The Israelites are enslaved, homeless, without hope. God has remembered them and wants to prepare them for redemption. The Israelites know only Egyptian power; they must be convinced of God's superior power as well as His love for them and His willingness to act for them.

Action is implied in the Name: unlike the other names for God, the Tetragrammaton is not a noun. It is a verb, and as such it implies action. By the ineffable Name itself God is telling Moses and the suffering Israelites that He will act on their behalf.

Moses wants to understand this great Being who introduces Himself, and when he naturally asks for God's name in Parashat Sh'mot, he really is asking for an explanation of God's special interest in Israel and His plan. Moses is actually asking tell me who you are; why do you care about us; what do you intend to do with me and my people and by what means will you act. God's response is simply *"Ehyeh asher Ehyeh"* another four-letter word spelled *Alef-Hei-Yod-Hei*. This is the first-person singular of the verb "to be" in Hebrew. The whole phrase is literally "I am who I am" or "I shall be who I shall be." This is not mysterious for the sense in these words is that God acts in this world. God uses this name (*Ehyeh*) again for Himself many years later while speaking to the prophet Nathan: *"Ehyeh* traveled in a tent and a tabernacle." (II Samuel 7:6)

When Moses recounts details about the Almighty in this Parashah, he obviously cannot use the first person singular because they might mistake him for God. He must use *Yod-Hei-Vav-Hei* which is the third person singular of the very "to be" even though it has a slightly different root from *Ehyeh*, God's name in the previous Parashah. (Cassuto, *Exodus,* pp. 37-38) Thus, the literal meaning of the Tetragrammaton could be all of the following: "He is" or "He will be" or "He lives" or "He causes to be." (*Jewish Encyclopedia,* p.5) Jews do not try to pronounce the Name because it is ineffable, beyond expression. Josephus warns his readers that God told Moses his name "concerning which it is not lawful for me to say any more." (in *Antiquities,* 2:12:4) What was Josephus worried about?

## 2. Why do Jews avoid saying the true name of God?

The third commandment "You shall not swear falsely by the name of the Lord…." (Ex 20:7) does not forbid the use of the Name, but in Parashat *Emor* in the Book of Leviticus (Lev 24:10-16) when the son of an Israelite woman curses others by using the Name of God, he is condemned to death for the curse as well as for speaking the Name. Nonetheless, it seems that during the First Temple times (11th century BCE to 6th Century BCE) lay people spoke and wrote the name without fear of blasphemy or disrespect to the Almighty. (Bickerman, pp. 262-266)

Avoidance and circumlocutions began with the restoration of the Temple at the end of the 6th century BCE according to the scholar Elias Bickerman. Bickerman says Jews were alarmed that magicians might put the four letters of God's name on amulets and some people were equating the written form of the Name with idols, violating the first commandment. (Bickerman, pp. 262-266) Later the sages explicitly forbade pronunciation of "the Name according to the letters." (Sanhedrin 91a) Only the High Priest could say the Name once a year on Yom Kippur. In addition, the rabbis of the Talmud warned that any document with the Name fully written on it might be thrown on a heap of garbage thereby desecrating the Name. (*Rosh Hashanah* 18b) Today no one really knows for sure how to pronounce the Name or to write it correctly with vowels.

Earlier, I asked "what's in a name?" We have to go beyond the literal meaning of the ineffable name to understand the answer. The Tetragrammaton looks simple, but within it the Israelites and their descendants, the Jews, discover for the first time the meaning of God's power and His relationship with Israelites and Jews as a people. Rashbam explains that the Tetragrammaton means action, protection, a force, a power that keeps promises. (*Commentators' Bible, Exodus,* on 6:2 p. 38) Umberto Cassuto expands further. The Name means "He will be with His creatures who need Him now and in the future." (Cassuto, *Exodus,* p. 38) Rabbi S.R. Hirsch summarizes: "All the development of Jewish history led to this moment." Israel had to start and rise up into a "[P]eople through God's creative call, so that the very existence of this People proclaims to the world *'Ani Adonai.'*" (*Hirsch – Exodus*, pp. 63-64) In other words, Revelation – before God's statements to Moses on Mount Sinai – inheres in the Name. Alter says "it was only on the threshold of God's intervention in history to liberate Israel that He revealed His unique name to the whole people." (Alter, p. 340, ftn. 3) Humble and full of awe before the power and love of God, Jews do not try to pronounce the Name.

## 3. Are there risks in certain forms of avoidance and the circumlocutions created to avoid saying the Name?

Yes, the first risk is that our fear of using the name can estrange us from the true text and meaning. During the communal blessings or the reading of the Torah the prayer leader or reader may hesitate even to say *Adonai* substituting for it *HaShem*. The second risk is confusion when different names are chosen. We substitute *Adonai* for the Tetragrammaton; then *Adinoi* for *Adonai* (Levy, p. 4). In English to avoid saying the masculine sounding "Lord" we go back to *Adonai*.

The third and greatest risk comes from the studious effort to avoid what seem to be gender references and then to go further by feminizing God's names. During communal prayer referring to God in feminine forms in, for example, blessings for the Sh'ma, blessings before and after reading the Torah or in *drashot* or talks about the weekly Parashah violate at least 1,500 years of custom and practice. In some prayer books or *siddurim* the Hebrew word *Adonai* is regularly put in the English translation of the Hebrew in order to avoid saying Lord, but, of course, that is exactly what *Adonai* means.

To avoid the English word Lord it makes as much sense to use the French *Monseigneur*.

References to God as "He" or "the Lord" in either Hebrew or in some other language are certainly masculine in form. Those who take the masculine reference literally are making a mistake. God transcends gender. There is much anthropomorphism in the Bible. In Exodus God says "I will stretch out my hand and strike Egypt." In Deuteronomy we read about "the mouth of the Lord." In fact, there is no "He"; there is no "mouth"; no "hand"; no "eyes" of God. God chose these figurative words to help humans situate and understand God within human frames of reference. The words cannot be changed.

Any arbitrary choice of feminine forms and names in communal prayer raises the gender issue where it has no place. These feminine forms are exclusive rather than inclusive because they force a literal gender interpretation on congregants. The intention behind the use of feminine forms is also at least partly secular, and it is disrespectful of the ineffable Name and the Revelation that the Name signifies. Egalitarianism is an important goal, but it can be achieved without violating sacred texts and traditions.

# 15

## *Bo*

✦

### *(Exodus 10:1-13:16)*

Egypt's kings and the Egyptian people are important for Jews throughout history. What can we learn by studying the Jewish relationship with Egypt and the Egyptians? What do we know about Egypt from the Bible, in addition to the fact that Israelites were enslaved there?

1.  Egypt is the only highly organized state in the Torah although, of course, there are other such political systems in the Prophets and Writings of the Bible. Egypt's government consisted of a monarch, advisors, an administration, a tax collection system about which I shall elaborate, a system for economic planning, a highly trained army, and a well defined territory.

2.  Egypt was a refuge. Because of famines in Canaan, Abraham sought refuge in Egypt; Jacob and his family settled there for the same reason. King Solomon's opponents, notably Jeroboam, exiled themselves to Egypt to escape death. The priest Onias settled in Egypt in the second century BCE after he had been denied the chief priesthood, and he established his own temple for the growing Jewish community there. The Christian Bible tells us that Joseph took his wife Mary and her son Jesus to Egypt because they feared Jesus would be killed. (Matthew 2:13) The Talmud says Egypt is destined to bring a gift to the Messiah. He will think not to accept it from them, but the Holy One blessed be He, will instruct him, 'Accept it from them – they furnished hospitality to My children in Egypt.'" (Pesachim 118b)

3.  Egypt is a place where Israelites prosper. Abram and Sarai carry riches back to Canaan; Jacob's descendants multiply to 600,000 men in fulfillment of God's promise "fear not to go down into Egypt; for I will there make of thee a great nation." (Gen 46:3)

Despite their condition of servitude the Israelites in this Parashah own cattle and land; their leader, Moses, had easy access to the king, and the Israelites received gold, silver, and clothing from the Egyptians when they departed.

The material attractions and the threat from Babylonia were such that by the end of the 7th century BCE and the beginning of the 6th century BCE Jews began to return to Egypt. They did not remember or know about the injunction not to return: "You must not go back that way again." (Deut 17:16) The invasion and destruction of the Temple by the Babylonians in 586 BCE drove more Jews to Egypt. The Jewish Diaspora prospered and grew in Egypt, and by the 3rd century BCE the Torah was translated into Greek there, and the Greek-speaking rulers, the Ptolemies, incorporated it, the Septuagint, into their judicial system. (Modrzejewski, p. 110)

The Jewish philosopher Philo (20 BCE – 50 CE) and his family thrived in Alexandria. A thousand years later Maimonides made Arab Egypt his home. The intellectual, economic and religious life of Jews in that land was vibrant and productive in the 11th, 12th, and 13th centuries as documents from the famous Cairo Geniza prove.

What is known about Egypt's rulers? The first king of Egypt mentioned in the Bible met Abram (Abraham) and Sarai (Sarah). He was punished with plagues for bringing Sarai into his palace, even though he was ignorant about her marital status. (Abram had pretended she was his sister.) The second is the monarch who hired Joseph to organize for the famine after Joseph interpreted his dreams. This king also saved Joseph's family by sending wagons to carry Joseph's father Jacob and his sons to Egypt. Many years later, a third king, who feared the increasingly numerous and successful Israelites as a possible security threat, ordered them into forced labor and decreed the murder of male newborns. He was succeeded by the king in this Parashah, the fourth king, who refused to let the Israelites go until the plagues forced him to do so.

We read about a fifth, in the Book of Kings. He had close diplomatic relations with King Solomon; he was also Solomon's father-in-law. Four more Egyptian monarchs are mentioned in various places in the Bible as they intervened in Israelite politics in various ways or as they themselves were in combat with the Babylonians.

History shows there was much that was good about Egypt and its government and in their behavior toward the Israelites. The Egyptian system had, however, one serious defect, namely, the fusion of secular and deific powers. Kings of Egypt claimed both secular and sacred power, and the Egyptian people worshipped their kings as deity while obeying them as the secular rulers of the state.

God's plan is to rescue His people and send them home to the Promised Land. He also has to rescue them from what must have been their partial assimilation into Egyptian culture and religion during their four centuries of residence there. They had kept parts of their identity, as I mentioned at the outset, but they were ignorant about the lives of their patriarchs and matriarchs. With the possible exception of the Levites, who were not enslaved, they knew nothing or practically nothing of the Covenant.

God knows it will not be easy to convince the Israelites of His power and to weaken the spiritual and political pretensions of the Egyptian king. It is necessary to harden the Pharaoh's heart, as the text says, in order to provide a demonstrable and powerful adversary who must be visibly defeated in the most humiliating ways possible. The Lord says: "You shall soon see what I will do to Pharaoh; he shall let them go because of a greater might...." (Ex 6:1) The combat thus begins.

In order to demonstrate to the Israelites and to the Egyptians who is the true Master of the Universe, God first manipulated symbols important to the Egyptians. In a scene where Moses and Aaron confront the mighty king God first transforms their wooden staffs into snakes which swallow snakes holy to the Egyptians. Then, the River Nile, which gives life to Egypt, was turned into blood. Worst of all from the king's perspective Moses is instructed to tell the king that the only purpose for letting the Israelites go is to allow them to worship God, a direct insult to the king who thinks there is no greater power than his own.

Moses never tells the king of Egypt that he wants the Israelites to be free from bondage so that they can go to the Promised Land. Moses only requests a sort of leave of absence from their work in order that they might make sacrifices to God at a distance of three days walk from the king's palace. In other words, the king is led to believe the Israelites will return.

After the king finally acquiesced to Moses' request following the horrors of the tenth and last plague, he realized the Israelites were actually fleeing the country for good. He sent his soldiers in pursuit up to the edge of the Sea of Reeds. Since throughout history a powerful Egypt consistently tried to extend its control northeast to Canaan and Syria, the destruction of an important part of the king's army in the waters of the Sea of Reeds, which had parted only long enough to let the Israelites pass through, freed the Promised Land from Egyptian influence. There was no military threat from Egypt for the duration of the 40-year period from the exodus to the crossing into the Promised Land, but Egypt did not, of course, disappear from the Bible.

God accepts the existence of secular states for the peoples of the earth. Even though the king of Egypt was the first-born, he did not die in the 10th plague, the death of the first-born.

Nor did God ever destroy the Egyptian state. Egypt continued to survive and even thrive at different points in its very long history. According to the prophet Jeremiah, although Egypt would be defeated on the battlefield by the Babylonians, "afterward she shall be inhabited again as in former days, declares the Lord." (Jer 46:26)

It was Joseph who helped Egypt maintain its preeminent status. He strengthened the Egyptian state during the seven years of plenty and the seven years of famine that we have read about. Centuries later other Jews served the state in similar ways. For example, Feldman has written that during the second century BCE four Jews served as commanders-in-chief of the Ptolemy armies. (Feldman, 1993, pp. 87-88) Subsequent to the Muslim conquest a convert from Judaism organized the finances of the state. (Goitein, Vol I, 1967, p. 33)

In summary, what can we learn about power from the history of Jewish relations with Egypt, the Egyptian kings and the people themselves?

1.  Egypt is the symbol of states which are both a threat and a refuge for the Jewish Diaspora. The potential threat to Jews posed by such states is loss of identity, oppression and death. Refuge means safety, prosperity and satisfaction of personal ambition.

2.  The king of Egypt – like all rulers – has to learn about the limits to his own power. When Moses first asked for permission for the Israelites to go to worship God, the king responded in a contemptuous manner: "Who is the Lord that I should heed Him and let Israel go? I do not know the Lord, nor will I let Israel go." (Ex 5:2) After the ten plagues the monarch said "Go worship the Lord…. And may you bring a blessing on Me also." (Ex 12:31) He has understood the power of God in spiritual matters, and he will soon understand that the true Master of the Universe can control the secular state if He chooses.

3.  What about the Egyptian people who have no power? In this Parashah, something positive is written about them. They and the king's advisors were "favorably disposed toward [the Israelites and Moses.]" (Ex 11:3), but they remain in the background. God's focus is on redeeming the Israelites and preparing them to play their role in human history. He knows it will be difficult to convince the Israelites to follow His plan for them. When Moses first tells them about their imminent release, "they would not listen to Moses, their spirits crushed by cruel bondage." (Ex 6:9) If they could have believed in God immediately, perhaps the Egyptian people would have been spared their suffering. Like the king, once the Israelites saw the plagues and the drowning of the army, they fully understood God's superior power; they broke into song: "The Lord is my strength and might. He is become my deliverance. This is my God, and I will

glorify Him; the God of my father, and I will exalt Him." (Ex 15:2) No further punishment for the Egyptian people was needed.

Some commentators say that the death of all Egyptians' firstborn was punishment of the Egyptians for their guilt. (Cf. Rashi on Ex 11:5-6) I do not see anything in the text of the Torah accusing the ordinary Egyptians of guilty behavior. These deaths were necessary to convince the king and to convince Israel of God's power in order that the Israelites might be freed to become God's obedient servants. Jews should, therefore, understand God's purpose in making the ordinary Egyptians suffer. If Jews doubt God's power; if Jews reject God's supremacy; and if Jews fail to observe the commandments, Jews are guilty of allowing others to suffer and die in vain.

# 16

## *B'shallach*

✦

### *(Exodus 13:17-17:16)*

In this Parashah we read that the king relented and permitted the Israelites to leave. The Hebrew *b'shallach* literally means he sent them away. He was glad to see them go to worship their God in return for some peace and quiet at home. But, when the monarch realized that Moses had deceived him and that the goal was to free the Israelites from bondage, he sent his soldiers in pursuit.

As soon as the Israelites saw the Egyptians coming, they despaired. Moses urged them to have courage. Miracles happened: a cloud separated the Israelites from the advancing army, and then the Sea of Reeds split apart to let the Israelites cross. As soon as the Israelites reached the other side, the water closed in on the troops drowning them. Finally, the Israelites expressed their "faith in the Lord and His servant Moses." (Ex 14:31) They sang.

Safe at last from the Egyptian enemy the Israelites moved into the wilderness of the present-day Sinai Peninsula. They began to suffer from hunger and the heat. In response the Lord sent bread, quail, manna and water. Suddenly the Amalekites attacked them. God condemned this gratuitous and vicious action and ordered Moses to write for posterity that God will ensure that the Amalekites will be destroyed and forgotten.

Here is a question: We know from Parashat *Sh'mot* that God remembered the Israelites and the Covenant between Himself and their ancestors, but do the Israelites remember God and the Covenant? Yes is the answer, of course. Here is the proof:

1. Despite four centuries in Egypt the Israelites have kept their Israelite identity, and their individual tribal identities. Awareness of identity also means that there is a certain tribal infrastructure or hierarchy

that Moses will be able to use in order to communicate with the population.

2.   Despite four centuries in Egypt they remembered the promises made to Joseph that his bones would be carried back to the ancestral homeland. It cannot be Moses who recalled the promise because he had been living alternately in the king's household and then in the Midianite household of his father-in-law. Others kept the memory of Joseph alive, and they told Moses to retrieve the bones. The fact that they knew where to find the bones means the location must have been some kind of shrine.

The words of the song within the Parashah are so important that the name of the Sabbath is *Shabbat Shirah* (the Sabbath of Song). When it is chanted in the synagogue, congregants are supposed to stand to honor the ancestors and to participate in the singing of this beautiful song of redemption.

Think about it. The Israelites, like any enslaved people, want their freedom. Freedom could have meant their integration into Egyptian society as Egyptians. The words of the song suggest that they do not want to be Egyptians; rather, they want to return to their special relationship with the Lord.

In these verses of praise the Israelites sing that they recognize or remember that the Lord "is my strength and might," (Ex 15:2) "my deliverance" "my God" who is to be exalted. "Who is like You, O Lord, among the celestials. Who is like You, majestic in holiness." (Ex 15:11) The Lord will bring the people to His own mountain, to a sanctuary, and "The Lord will reign forever and ever." (Ex 15:18) In this way the Israelites exalt God; they express their faith and loyalty in God. This is a song of gratitude to the Almighty for remembering and redeeming them. They reaffirm their Israelite identity.

The lesson to the modern world is clear and simple. If after 400 years in Egypt and after being enslaved the Israelites can remember and begin their return to the faith of their ancestors, Jews living in the Diaspora as free men and women should be able to do the same.

# 17

## *Yitro*

◆

### *(Exodus 18:1-20:23)*

Who is Yitro, and why is he important? God is very clear about Yitro's identity, namely, he is a Midianite priest, who is Moses' father-in-law. He is not an Israelite, but he gives Moses some very important advice about governance.

After he notices how much time Moses spends judging disputes among the people, Yitro makes some suggestions: You are the intermediary between the Lord and the people, but you must find "capable men who fear God, trustworthy men....and let them judge the people at all times. Have them bring every major dispute to you, but let them decide every minor dispute themselves. Make it easier for yourself by letting them share the burden with you." (Ex 18: 21-22) In other words, Yitro recommends decentralizing authority.

Moses accepts this advice because he knows that the Midianites and their priests have considerable experience in administrative matters. God is Moses' teacher, but Moses can learn from other peoples, too. This Midianite's advice is given shortly before the Theophany – the giving of the commandments by God to Moses, commandments which will distinguish Israel from the other peoples of the world.

Yitro is not the only non-Israelite who teaches our people or who brings something to our people. Boaz marries Ruth, a Moabite. Ruth brings Moabite monarchical traditions which David, her descendant, will need. Moreover, the Tanakh tells us about the help offered to King Solomon by the King of Tyre and about the benevolence of Cyrus, the King of Persia, who ended the exile of the Jews. God's commandments to the Israelites in Parashat *Yitro* set the Israelites apart, building a type of fence between them and other peoples, but throughout Israelite and Jewish history the interaction, the mutual learning between Jews and others never ceases.

Similarly, we learn from the *Ethics of the Fathers*, in the Talmud, that "the men of the Great Assembly" said it was necessary to "make a *seyag* [fence] around the Torah." (Urbach, *The Halakhah,* p. 7). The purpose of the fence was to prevent the violation of the commandments, but it was not meant to prevent adaptation to new circumstances. The outside world and changing times would affect the nature of obedience.

Rabbinical *takkanot* (from "repair") as early as the third century BCE, "were regulations intended to correct situations in a positive manner." For example, soldiers were not supposed to fight on the Sabbath, but they were allowed to take up arms to defend the people when the enemies attacked on the Sabbath. "*Gezzerot* (from "decree") were "prohibitive and restrictive." The rabbis said Jews must not raise pigs – pigs are only explicitly forbidden in the Torah as food – and not to study "Greek wisdom" – meaning philosophy and science. (Urbach, *The Halakhah,* pp. 7–8, 28-29) These two types of rabbinical decisions resulted in adaptation of the Torah to new circumstances.

We may associate the *takkanot* with modern Judaism which encourages Jews to adapt to the world as it is. We associate the *gezzerot* with *Haredi* Judaism (usually called "ultra orthodox") which isolates Jews from the world around them.

Yes, Torah is meant to be a fence between the Children of Israel and the rest of the world, and the Jews are instructed to place a fence around Torah to prevent change. In both cases the fence stands, but it is porous in the sense that it allows for adaptation, for mutually beneficial currents between the Jews and other peoples in the times they live. The Torah and the Jews are not reified; both the Torah and the Jews maintain their vitality and relevance for all time.

# 18

## *Mishpatim*

◆

### *(Exodus 21:1 – 24:18)\**

Shakespeare makes his character Shylock commit four secular mistakes in his dealings with Antonio, the merchant of Venice, mistakes which are also violations of Jewish law: First, he foregoes the normal and expected interest on his loan of 3,000 ducats cosigned by Antonio, and says he prefers to take a pound of Antonio's flesh in the unlikely case of default. Second, when Antonio unexpectedly does default on the loan, Shylock wants to cut a pound of flesh from near the merchant's heart which will, of course, kill the man. Thirdly, Shylock rejects the eloquent appeal for mercy; and fourth, he insists rigidly on the letter of the law.

If Shakespeare had known more about the Torah and the Talmud, he would never have had Shylock, an observant and committed Jew, make these mistakes. Nevertheless, his treatment of Shylock shows the depth of his understanding of human character and emotions. Shakespeare creates an immortal character even though "there are times when one might wish it were otherwise," (in the excellent words of John Gross, p. 209) Shylock is at the same level of tragic greatness as Othello and King Lear whose own mistakes lead to their destruction. If Shakespeare meant to be anti-Jewish in the *Merchant of Venice*, we can also accuse him of hating blacks in *Othello* and of despising the elderly in *King Lear*. The greatest writer in the history of English literature is not showing an anti-Jewish bias in *The Merchant of Venice*, although his story has been widely used in anti-Semitic screeds since the play was produced. I shall explain my conclusion in due course.

First, the issue of interest on a loan. We read in Parashat *Mishpatim* that "If you lend money to My people, to the poor among you, do not act toward them as a creditor: exact no interest from them." (Ex 22:24) Implicit here is the permission to require interest from a non-Jew. The distinction between lending to Jews and non-Jews is made clearer in Deuteronomy. Moses tells the Israelites: "You shall not deduct interest from loans to your countrymen, whether in money or food or anything else that can be deducted as interest; but you may deduct interest from loans to foreigners." (Deut 23:20-21) According to Maimonides, the Jewish lender must require interest on loans to non-Jews: He writes in *Mishneh Torah* (*The Code of Maimonides*) "it is an affirmative commandment to lend money at interest to a foreigner."(*Code*, p. 93)

Second, Shylock's earlier friendly posture changes by the time the loan is due, and he means to kill Antonio which, of course, is a violation of the sixth commandment, You shall not murder. Something has happened in Shylock's life which almost turns him into a murderer. I shall explain that later. Third, in one of the great speeches of English literature, Portia, pretending to be a legal specialist, asks Shylock to reconsider his demand for the pound of flesh:

"The quality of mercy is not strained,
It droppeth as the gentle rain from heaven
Upon the place beneath; it is twice blessed
It blesseth him that gives and him that takes;"

Shylock refuses, thereby violating instructions from the prophet Micah and various Talmudic injunctions. Micah said: "He has told you, oh man, what is good and what does the Lord require of you, but to do justice, and to love mercy, and to walk humbly with your God." (Micah 6:8) According to the Talmud, "he who is merciful to others, mercy is shown to him by Heaven, while he who is not merciful to others, mercy is not shown to him by Heaven." (Shabbat 151b and see Makkot 24a)

Fourthly, when Shylock shouts, "My deeds upon my head! I crave the law, the penalty and forfeit of my bond," we realize that Shakespeare is ignorant of the Talmud.

An observant Jew knows that law must be interpreted and reinterpreted in changed circumstances, and when Shakespeare has him say: "I crave the law," Shakespeare is distorting Jewish tradition, culture and law. Unfortunately, these words resonate through the centuries in the calumnies of the anti-Semites of all stripes.

The association of Jews with usury precedes Shakespeare, of course, and has been used to mock and degrade and kill Jews. The word "usury" has no negative connotation as its original meaning is simply the use of money. The money we pay to live in the house of another person is "rent." The money we pay to use the money of someone else is "usury."(See Bentham, pp. 13-14) The negative connotation has developed in Islamic and Christian writings: According to the Koran (Sura IV: 160-161), "And [Jews] taking usury though indeed they were forbidden it and their devouring the property of people falsely; and We have prepared for the unbelievers from among them a painful chastisement." From the fifth century C.E., the pope prohibited usury based on the words of the Gospel according to Luke 6:35 – "lend, expecting nothing in return." (Cf. Buckley, p. 107) But, lending for interest was obviously so widespread in the church that from the 12th century, Christian moneylenders taking usury were threatened with excommunication. Shakespeare's own father was a money lender among other things. (Gross, p. 59)

Jews who were excluded from owning land and exercising most professions in Christian countries were allowed to lend money for interest, and Shakespeare knew it. The Protestant Reformation legitimized usury for its followers. The Roman Catholic Church lifted its ban in 1917 and made an artificial distinction between the word "interest" which they said is reasonable return on a loan and "usury" which is excessive return on a loan. (See Buckley, pp. 132, 152-159) Despite these changes in Christianity, the negative association of Jews with money lending seems well imbedded in the Christian mind during Shakespeare's time and until the present.

Modern capitalism would be impossible without interest and credit, but in a fit of grotesque hypocrisy, Max Weber, defender of capitalism, wrote that "Jewish capitalism was speculative pariah-capitalism, while the Puritan was bourgeois organization of labour." (cited by Buckley, p. 271) No one can match the vile language of Karl Marx, the quintessential self-loathing Jew, who consistently referred to a panoply of exploiters as Shylocks. (See Gross, pp. 343- 44).

The play itself has always been popular among anti-Semites, but an anti-Jewish bias cannot explain the fact that the first Shakespeare play to be performed in both China and Japan was the *Merchant of Venice*. The second Shakespeare play to be translated into Yiddish was the *Merchant of Venice*. Habima Theater, in Tel Aviv, produced it in Hebrew in 1936. (Gross, pp. 250, 276, 282) It is simply a great work of art.

Who remembers that Antonio, not Shylock, is the merchant of Venice? Shylock is unforgettable even though he "is present in only five of the play's twenty scenes...." (Gross, p. 64) Shakespeare's depiction of Shylock's emotions and failings are brilliant, and he overshadows everyone else. Shylock is at times mean and vengeful, loving and affectionate. "[H]e is also remarkable for pride, energy, quickness in argument. He has an abrasive sense of humor and a large capacity for being hurt." (Gross, p. 64)

To understand this man let's look at the reason for the peculiar pound of flesh clause in the original agreement between Shylock and the merchant of Venice and then at the reasons for Shylock's desire to kill Antonio. Shylock is an alien in Venice, the member of a despised minority, who is nonetheless a necessary fixture in the business community. He and Antonio have known each other for years. Antonio has lent money in the past at no interest, partly to undermine Shylock, and when he sees Shylock in public, he regularly abuses him by spitting on him and mocking him with words we can guess. All his life, Shylock must accept the insults and worse. So, why would Shylock decline to take the regular and expected interest on the loan to his enemy? He knows according to the laws of Torah and Venice that he has a right to interest, and even an obligation to take interest, but Shakespeare is telling us that he is trying to ingratiate himself with the merchant of Venice.

There has to be some penalty for non-payment written into such agreements, and Shylock thinks of the most absurd penalty of all, namely, a pound of human flesh. He says to the audience: "what should I gain By the exaction of the forfeiture? A pound of man's flesh taken from a man is not so estimable, profitable neither, As flesh of muttons, beefs or goats. I say to buy his favor I extend this friendship." (Act I:3:160-165) In other words, he wants to be accepted as a man, like everyone else in Venice. He thinks that Antonio and the other Christians may change their negative views about him and the Jewish community. Antonio understands the gesture very well and responds with what he considers to be the highest compliment: "Hie thee, gentle Jew, The Hebrew will turn Christian; he grows kind." (Act I: 3:174-175) The melancholy truth is that trying to buy the favor of someone who hates you for who you are is a futile business indeed.

Time passes, and the ships that Antonio has backed are lost at sea. He is unable to repay the loan which he has guaranteed. Others come forward to offer Shylock the money Antonio owes him - even more than the original 3,000 ducats - but he refuses. His deep hatred for Antonio boils to the surface, and he wants to kill him and probably any other Christian who gets in his way. Why is this ordinarily self- controlled man suddenly so enraged?

The answer is clear to me. In the period of time between the signing of the agreement and Antonio's default, Jessica, Shylock's only child, rejects her widowed father and the Jewish people; she is ashamed of him, saying: "But though I am a daughter to his blood, I am not to his manners." (Act II: 4:18-19) She elopes with a Christian man, Lorenzo, and declares her desire to become a Christian. She steals money and jewels from her father, including a ring that Shylock's late wife had given him before they were married. He hears from a Jewish friend that Jessica has traded the ring in Genoa for a monkey. (Act 3:2:111-116)

Shylock wants revenge for the loss of his daughter and for the years of insult and humiliation. How can he think clearly? How can he remember Jewish law? How can he show mercy when no mercy or respect has ever been shown to him and his people? He is totally overwhelmed by rage.

Shylock admits the desire for revenge for Antonio's lack of respect and abusive behavior toward him saying: "and what is his reason? I am a Jew." Shylock then takes on the anti-Semites full force: "Hath not a Jew eyes? Hath not a Jew hands, organs, dimensions, senses, affections, passion? Fed with the same food, hurt with the same weapons, subject to the same diseases, healed by the same means, warmed and cooled by the same winter and summer as a Christian is? If you prick us, do we not bleed? If you tickle us, do we not laugh? If you poison us, do we not die? And if you wrong us, shall we not revenge? If we are like you in the rest, we will resemble you in that." (Act 3:1:55-65)

Without Shylock, this play is a light comedy peopled with forgettable shallow characters. Shakespeare created a tragic character as great as Othello, Lear and Hamlet. Here is a man who is forced to lend money because other professions are closed to Jews. Here is a man who is an alien in Venice; who is despised and mocked by his Christian contemporaries; who is nevertheless dedicated to his community and family but is betrayed by his daughter and whose rage leads him to challenge an unforgiving power and to violate Jewish law. Crushed by his adversaries and condemned by the Duke of Venice to convert to Christianity, Shylock is isolated and feels unwell. He goes home and says no more. Shakespeare gave it to him to have said it all.

* Published in a slightly different form in *Jewish Bible Quarterly,* Vol 35, No. 3, 2007, pp. 187 – 191. Published here with permission from JBQ.

# 19

## *T'rumah*

✦

## *(Exodus 25:1-27:19)*

God decides there has to be some place to put the tablets on which Moses has inscribed the commandments, and there must be a tangible sign of God's presence among the Israelites. God, therefore, orders Moses to construct a portable Tabernacle which will hold an ark containing the laws. In addition, the Israelites must build a table for bread, a lampstand or Menorah, a tent of cloth, a curtain, and a wooden altar for the Tabernacle. The materials necessary to construct this Tabernacle will come from the people who will give offerings - *t'rumah*, the name of this Parashah.

The materials include gold, silver, copper, yarns which are blue, purple and crimson, fine linen, goats' hair, tanned ram skins, acacia wood, oil, spices and various jewels. The most frequently named color is blue. The Biblical and Talmudic name for this particular blue is *techelet*. The Tabernacle will have a curtain of blue, purple and crimson yarns which will serve as "a screen for the entrance..." (Ex 26:36)

In Parashat *T'tzavveh* we read that the breastplate of the high priest "shall be held in place by a cord of blue..." (Ex 28:28) We read about this color blue again in chapter 15:38 of Numbers: "Speak unto the children of Israel, and bid them make fringes in the corners of their garments....putting upon the fringe of each corner a thread of blue." [*techelet*]. We also read about this color in the Book of Esther. After Haman's defeat, Mordechai goes out in garments of blue. ( Esther 8:15) The prophet Jeremiah says that elites of the nations wear blue. (See Jer. 10:9).

The true *techelet* dye is made from a species of snail, but the method of dye production was lost after the upheavals of the first century of the Common Era. A few years ago, Israeli scientists found the snail and have begun producing *techelet* again for the fringes on the prayer shawl or *tallit*.

My question is what is so special about this particular color blue for the Jewish people? Our *tallit*, or prayer shawl, often has blue stripes; the flag of Israel – imitating the colors and design of the *tallit* – is blue and white. In short, we use the color blue for many purposes. Other religious communities value different colors: Muslims like green. Mohammad's banners were green, and in the Koran, one reads that in heaven the believers will wear "green robes of fine silk" (Sura 18:31) In the Christian Bible, one reads that Roman soldiers put a purple robe on Jesus before the crucifixion. (See John 19:2) During the period preceding Easter many churches and Christian clergy wear purple vestments. Hindus prefer the color saffron.

The Zohar explains that "The sea was dyed with that [*techelet*] which symbolizes the Throne of Judgment." (*Zohar* II: 149b) Referring specifically to the instructions in this week's Parashah, the Zohar says: "The blue employed in the work of the Tabernacle symbolized the mystery of the upper world." (*Zohar* II: 226b) Similarly, in the Zohar we read that a blue thread bound the breastplate to the ephod of the high priest because blue is an "all-uniting color." (Zohar, II:231a)

I think the Biblical reference to blue gives us a colorcoding system like the ones we use in our daily lives – on our national flags, in the colors we choose to paint our houses or the color of a suit, a tie, a blouse, a dress to identify who we are, and what we stand for. In other words, this symbol helps us find our way to what we need, namely, the commandments; it serves to unify us as one Jewish people; it reminds us of our collective identity and history; it makes us feel good about ourselves. We Jews, today, need this help more than our ancestors did because there is no Tabernacle on which to focus our attention; instead we can look up at the blue sky every day to remind ourselves of God and His works.

# 20

## *T'tzavveh*

✦

## *(Exodus 27:20 – 30:10)*

In this Parashah, Moses receives more detailed instructions about the Tabernacle and its maintenance. The Lord begins by telling Moses to command the Israelites to bring "clear oil of beaten olives for lighting, for kindling lamps regularly...." (Ex 27:20). The word here for "command" or "instruct" is *t'tzavveh,* the name of the Parashah.

Aaron and his sons will be priests. They must wear certain clothes and ornaments which the Torah describes with great precision. Moses will consecrate them by anointing Aaron and his sons with oil, by sacrificing a bull at the altar, then a ram. After the sanctification of the Tabernacle or Tent of Meeting, and the altar and after the consecration of Aaron and his sons, the Lord says, "I will abide among the Israelites..." (Ex 29:45) Lastly, Moses must build "an altar for burning incense." (Ex 30:1)

I want to say a word about one of the products which is frequently mentioned and often used for ritual purposes, namely, the olive and olive tree. Olives grow along the Mediterranean littoral, and the peoples living in that area use its oil for cooking and other important purposes. Archaeological sites in Israel reveal oil presses around ancient homes and towns. It is the oil of olives that will burn in the aforementioned Tabernacle lamps, and the oil used for anointing the priests is part olive oil and part spices. The wood of the tree was fashioned into many useful items for daily life. Solomon used olive wood for doors in the First Temple. According to Nechemiah (8:15), people should construct the Sukkah with olive branches along with myrtle branches and palm branches.

The olive tree also has symbolic value for Jews and for many other peoples some of whom may never have seen an olive tree. The expression, offering an olive branch, means to strive for peace with former enemies, and it is used even in places where there are no olive trees. It is possible that this symbolic association stems from the story of No-ach and the ark. No-ach sent a dove from the ark to test whether the flood had abated. When the dove returned with an olive branch, No-ach knew that he would soon be able to leave the ark. We could conclude from this story that the olive branch has come to represent the reconciliation of God and humanity. (Gen 8:11)

For people from the period of the Bible, the olive was one of the staples of life. It became a symbol of the relationship of the children of Israel and the land. The prophet Micah warns the Jews that when they disobey the commandments, "you shall tread the olives, but you shall not anoint yourself with oil; you shall tread grapes, but shall not drink wine." (Micah 6:15) The Promised Land is said to contain wheat, barley, vines, fig trees, pomegranates, olive oil and honey. (Deut 8:8) For the prophet Jeremiah, the olive tree serves as a symbol of Israel or its leaders. (Jer 11:16) Similarly we read in Psalm 52:10 "But I am like a green olive tree in the house of God." And in Psalm 128:3 children are like "olive shoots around your table."

What is the importance of this discussion of olives? Lawyers say that "the devil is in the details" particularly when they are talking about a contract. The minutiae can become more important than the grand outlines.

All of the details in the Torah are important, but there is a danger in focusing excessively on the details. Rabbi Tarfon, quoted in the Mishnah, says that only olive oil will do for Sabbath lights, no matter where Jews live, but other sages said that where it is not available other oils – even fish oil – will be acceptable. (Shabbat 24b) The sages are warning us not to be overwhelmed by details which can distract us from the broader obligations of the Covenant with God. We must try to understand and obey every word of Torah, but if by following every detail, we lose sight of the requirements of deeds of loving kindness, prayer, study and justice, we risk losing our relationship with the Almighty.

# 21

## *Ki-Tissa*

✦

## *(Exodus 30:11-34:35)*

The Lord finishes His instructions to Moses with the following command: "When you take a census of the Israelite people...." The words "When you take" correspond to the Hebrew words: *ki-tissa,* the name of this Parashah. The census served many functions among them taxation and military service. In the continuation of the Parashah, Moses received further commands regarding the rituals of the priesthood. The Torah also reemphasized the importance of Shabbat. The Torah then returns to the event which is the focal point of the book of Exodus: "He [God] gave Moses the two tablets of the Pact, stone tablets inscribed with the finger of God." (Ex 31:18)

During Moses' absence from the people while he was atop Mount Sinai, the Israelites had become restive and anxious. They demanded that Aaron make for them "a god who shall go before us, for that man Moses, who brought us from the land of Egypt – we do not know what has happened to him." (Ex 32:1) In response, Aaron meekly molded an image of gold that looked like a calf. An altar was built before it and the people made sacrifices to it, thereby violating the commandments: "You shall have no other gods besides Me. You shall not make for yourself a sculptured image [and] You shall not bow down to them or serve them." (Ex 20: 2-5) God saw what they had been doing and told Moses that He was going to destroy the people on account of this transgression. Moses pleaded with God not to destroy the people for their infidelity. God relented, and Moses descended to face the people.

When Moses, accompanied by Joshua, saw the calf and the Israelites dancing in front of it, "he became enraged; and he hurled the tablets from his hands and shattered them at the foot of the mountain." (Ex 32:19). He punished the Israelites by grinding the golden calf into dust, mixing the dust with water, and forcing the Israelites to drink it. After God meted out other punishments, He instructed Moses to carve two more tablets and to ascend Mt. Sinai once again in order to receive the commandments. My question is: Why did Moses destroy the first pair of tablets? How could he dare destroy what God had inscribed beginning with His own holy name, "Anochi Adonai?"(Ex 20:2)

Rabbis have different explanations for Moses' extraordinary action. According to *Pesikta Rabbati*, Moses and Joshua debated what to do with the first set of tablets after observing the incident of the golden calf. They thought that if they returned the tablets to the Almighty, He would destroy Israel; on the other hand, they knew they could not present the tablets to the Israelites who had just violated the commandments inscribed on them. Consequently, the two men just let the tablets slip out of their hands. (*Pesikta Rabbati*, 20:2, p. 404) Centuries later, the Spanish commentator, Abraham Ibn Ezra compared the destruction of the tablets to tearing up a contract which had been violated. (Ibn Ezra on Ex 32:18) Rabbi Elie Munk recorded a tradition that "the Tablets slipped from Moses' hands because the letters suddenly flew away on their own, and consequently, the Tablets grew heavy like a body without a soul." (*The Call…Exodus,* on 32:19,p. 455)

In my opinion, this episode shows that the once diffident Moses has now become the resolute and courageous leader that God knew he could become by the force of his intellect and personality. Previous Parashot have focused on Aaron and his descendants and their role as priests. We might have concluded that the priesthood would become the preeminent authority for the Israelites for all time. We now understand from this Parashah that Moses is a stronger figure than Aaron, his elder brother, who held the position of high priest. Aaron proved to be a weaker leader, who seemed to succumb meekly to the people's desire for an idol. Moses' actions tell us we can live without priests, but we cannot live without strong secular leaders and teachers.

In later Parashot we can compare leaders such as Joshua with Pinchas, the priest; in other books of the Bible we can compare King David and King Solomon with priestly authority. In the Books of Samuel we see the importance of a judge and kingmaker. The prophets play a powerful role as they speak to the kings and people about their failings, and as they remind Israel what God demands of them.

The priesthood was established as an intermediary between the Almighty and Israel. The High Priest had an essential role, for example, on the Day of Atonement, Yom Kippur, in reestablishing the special relationship between God and His people. But, early in our history we learn from the story of Aaron that the priests are fallible, and Israel can survive without them.

# 22

## *Va-yak-hel*

✦

### *(Exodus 35:1-38:20)*

At the end of the last Parashah, we read that after the disaster of the golden calf and the destruction of the tablets Moses returned to Mount Sinai for another 40 days and 40 nights. At the beginning of this Parashah, Moses has descended again to face the people. The text reads: "Moses then convoked the whole Israelite community….." (Ex 35:1) The Hebrew for convoked is *va-yak-hel* - the name of the Parashah.

Moses presents the people with the second set of tablets containing the commandments, and he asks the people for donations – "gifts for the Lord" – in order to construct the mobile Tabernacle.

God instructs Bezalel, the main architect, to make "two cherubim of gold" for the cover of the ark. The Torah states that "he made them of hammered work, at the two ends of the cover…." over the Holy Ark. These cherubim "had their wings spread out above, shielding the cover with their wings. They faced each other; the faces of the cherubim were turned toward the cover." (Ex 37:7-9) In Parashat *T'rumah* the Lord tells Moses that He the Lord will speak "from between the two cherubim which are upon the ark…" (Ex 25:22)

We may have forgotten that these creatures appear early in Torah. After Adam and Eve were expelled from the Garden of Eden, God placed a flaming sword and cherubim at the east of the Garden to prevent their return. (See Genesis 3:24). In this Parashah, they continue their role as guards. They were so important that Solomon installed them in the First Temple. In the Book of I Kings (8:6) we read: "And the priests brought in the ark of the covenant of the Lord to His place, to the sanctuary of the house, to the most holy place, under the wings of the cherubim." The prophet Ezekiel refers to these images many times saying, for example, that they carry God on a throne. (Ez 10:15-

20) In Psalm 99 we read: "The Lord reigns; let the people tremble. He sits between the cherubim..." (Ps 99:1)

What did they look like? Rashi explains that they had, "the form of a child's face." (Rashi on Exodus 25:18). We already know they had wings; and they were part of the cover of the ark. In Solomon's Temple they were carved from olive wood and covered with gold.

These images are confusing. In the previous Parashah we read that the Israelites were punished for making a calf out of gold soon after the commandments forbade them from sculpting any images; yet, in this Parashah they are commanded to make figures out of gold. Why is it that the Israelites must sculpt these cherubim for the Tabernacle and Temple but they are forbidden to sculpt the calf?

One possible answer is that the Israelites had intended for the golden calf to replace Moses or perhaps even God, whereas the cherubim were made to symbolize God's presence, to remind Israel of God's message contained within the Ark.

Cherubim were intended to be servants of the Lord as are angels who appear in the Torah from time to time. I think we must return to the story of the Garden of Eden to understand the significance of the cherubim. God punished Adam and Eve because they ate fruit which gave them knowledge of good and bad. Yet, God gave knowledge through Torah. Similarly, God punished the Israelites for making the golden calf; yet, God gave them the golden cherubim.

It seems that God does not want humans to discover knowledge for its own sake; knowledge has a purpose, mainly obedience to the Almighty's will. Similarly, God fears that we shall worship images we have fashioned. He will tell us what images to sculpt and what to do with them. They will be reminders of God's will and symbolic protectors of God's will at the entrance of the Garden of Eden and over the Holy Ark.

It seems to me that from the beginning of time we humans have tried to seize the initiative from God in order to gain and use knowledge and to manipulate the material world in ways that suit us. God gave us rules and a purpose, but resistance to them never ceases because of the nature of human beings who are intelligent because God made them intelligent. God often seems surprised by human decisions and choices, and He gets angry, but God created humans in His own image. He might have suspected the outcome.

# 23

## *P'kudei*

◆

## *(Exodus 38:21 – 40:38)*

In this last Parashah of the Book of Exodus, we read the inventory – *p'kudei,* the name of the Parashah – the inventory of the materials used in the mobile Tabernacle.

Bezalel and Oholiab, the principal contractors, used a total of "29 talents and 730 shekels" of gold (38:24) and 100 talents and 1,775 shekels of silver. (Ex 38:25) Talent and shekel were units of weight – the talent was the equivalent of about 24 kilograms while the shekel weighed approximately 11 grams.

Some years on this Sabbath we also read the announcement that men would pay a tax of one-half shekel of silver the first of the following month of Nissan (Shabbat Shekalim, Exodus 30: 11 – 16). The subject matter of this commandment is discussed in the tractate or treatise known as *Shekalim* in the Jerusalem Talmud. In this tractate, the rabbis explain how this annual silver offering was carried out and what its purpose was. What do these precious metals, particularly gold, signify?

Judaism shares with Hinduism and ancient Egypt a great respect for gold. What is special about gold? It does not change by oxidation and seems to last forever. It is also soft and malleable and is consequently easy to shape into any form, including, unfortunately, a golden calf, as we have read. It is very beautiful. It shines, and its color reminds us of the life-giving sun. In the last few Parashot, God instructs Moses about the use of gold in the Tabernacle and in the high priest's garments. Solomon also used large quantities of gold in the construction of the First Temple in Jerusalem.

Where does the Bible tell us that gold came from? Sheba, Havilah, Ophir and Tarshish, but one is not sure where these places are. In the Torah, we read that Abram brought gold back from Egypt (Gen 13:2) The king of Egypt gave Joseph a necklace of gold, presumably as a sign of Joseph's authority. The Egyptians lent gold to the Israelites who were leaving under Moses' leadership.

King David's military victories filled the coffers with gold, silver and bronze, an alloy which is frequently mentioned in Torah. The Israelites who returned to Jerusalem after the Babylonian exile were supposed to receive silver and gold gifts from other peoples in order to rebuild the Temple, according to the orders of the Persian king, Cyrus. (Ezra 1:4-6)

Gold and silver have negative connotations, too. A major and troubling example is the Christian misunderstanding about the half-shekel of silver that we read about this Sabbath. Gospel writers, Matthew and Mark, claim that Jesus overthrew the tables of the moneychangers at the Temple. These two men misinterpreted the purpose of the moneychangers which was to take the coins of Jews coming from various parts of the Diaspora where the silver half-shekel was not available. These money changers performed a useful function by arranging for the pilgrims who came to Jerusalem to exchange their coins for the proper silver coins. Thus, the visitors could fulfill this yearly mitzvah. As such, the moneychangers and their task were important, and I doubt very much that anyone who understood the need for their services would object to their money changing activities.

Gold can also have a negative connotation in the Jewish Bible. In Lamentations, we read that when Israel is punished "gold becomes dim." (Lam 4:1) The rabbis in the Mishnah tell us "the law of the mouth is better unto Me [the Lord] than thousands of pieces of gold and silver." (Avot, Ch. 6, Baraita 9) King David says to the Lord: "I prefer the teaching You proclaimed to thousands of gold and silver pieces." (Psalm 119:72)

Yes, gold and silver are important, and God wants gold in His holy house and silver for the maintenance of Jewish institutions. But, everything God tells us throughout Torah is that our loyalty to God and our ethical relations with other human beings are more precious to Him than the most beautiful metals.

# VA-YIKRA/LEVITICUS

# 24

## *Va-yikra*

♦

## *(Leviticus 1:1-5:26)*

The mobile Tabernacle, whose construction we have been reading about the last couple of Parashot, is now ready for the animal and grain sacrifices to be performed there. At the beginning of this Parashah, we read that in order to explain the various sacrifices, God "called to Moses" – *va-yikra el Moshe.* The word *va-yikra* meaning "called" marks the name of the third book of the Torah, also called Leviticus. In addition, when this Sabbath falls just before Purim, it is also known as *Shabbat Zachor* because we read as *Maftir* Deuteronomy 25:17-19. This Torah reading recounts the deeds of the tribe of Amalek which sought to destroy Israel. Haman, the villain of the story of Purim, is a descendant of Amalek; he also attempts to destroy Israel.

We learn in this portion that there are three types of sacrifices. The first is the "burnt offering" or *olah*, an animal offering totally consumed by flames; second, the grain offering or *minchah*, semolina wheat mixed with olive oil. The priests offer a small portion of this mixture to God, and the priests eat the rest. The third is the Sacred Gift of Greeting or well being offering known as the *zevach shelamim.* This is an animal sacrifice only part of which is offered to God through burning. The priests and the donors eat the remainder. Purposes of sacrifices include pleasing the Almighty with the aroma, drawing close to God by sharing a meal with God and expiation for inadvertent sins of commission and of omission.

The procedures for sacrifices are very detailed, particularly concerning the blood of the animals. For the burnt offering, the priests were to "offer the blood, dashing the blood against all sides of the altar which is at the entrance of the Tent of Meeting." (Lev 1:5) When a priest unwittingly errs, a bull was to be slaughtered; and the blood was sprinkled "seven times before the Lord, in front of the curtain of the Shrine. The priest shall [then] put some of the blood on the horns of the altar of aromatic incense…and all the rest of the

75

bull's blood he shall pour out at the base of the altar of burnt offering...." (Lev 4:6-7) What does blood signify in Jewish tradition?

After Cain killed Abel, God said to him: "The voice of your brother's blood cries to me from the ground." (Gen 4:10) In Parashat *No-ach*, God announced to all of humanity that they may not eat the blood of animals for blood is the animals' life. Moses repeats this injunction in Deuteronomy. (Deut12:23) He warns the Israelites that when they eat meat, they must "make sure that you do not partake of the blood; for the blood is the life, and you must not consume the life with the flesh...." Kosher meat has blood of the animal removed from it.

As we think about Passover we remember another significance of blood: lamb's blood was placed on the doorposts to protect those inside the house from the last and most terrible plague in Egypt. When God saw the blood, He passed over those houses thus saving the inhabitants from death of the firstborn.

What can we conclude about the significance of blood in Jewish practice and tradition? First, it is a purging or cleansing agent for the altar. Second, it represents the life force or soul which humans are forbidden to consume. Jewish concerns about the blood of every being are an expression of a deep reverence for life. Does this reverence contradict the injunction on *Shabbat Zachor* to remember and to destroy all the Amalekites who have threatened Israel with destruction? And how can we applaud the killing of the evil Haman and his family on Purim? The answer is that reverence for life also includes the defense of Jewish lives.

# 25

## Tzav

♦

## (Leviticus 6:1-8:36)

The Book of *Vayikra* - Leviticus as the Jews of Alexandria, Egypt called it – seems divorced from our experiences and obligations. It seems rather like a manual for the use of priests and Levites. This Parashah, *Tsav*, which means "command," begins with God telling Moses to "command" the priests about the conduct of Temple sacrifices and the maintenance of their holiness and purity.

What is so special about the Levites and Kohanim? And, do the instructions imparted to them have any relevance for us?

In the Book of Numbers God commanded Moses regarding those who should serve in the sanctuary in the desert. Originally, the first born of all tribes were to serve in this role: "all the first born are mine, for on the day I struck all the first born in Egypt, I consecrated to Me all the first born in Israel...." (Num 3:13) God, however, eventually preferred the whole tribe of Levites. God commanded: "I have taken the Levites...instead of all the first born....therefore, the Levites shall be Mine." (Numbers 3:12) What is so special about this tribe?

Levi was the third son of Jacob and Leah. Levi then had three sons: Gerson, Kohath and Merari. Kohath had four sons, including Amram. Amram and his wife Jochebed had three children, namely, Aaron, Miriam and Moses. Only the descendants of Aaron, the Levite, are priests; the other Levites are assistants, musicians, judges, and teachers in Jerusalem and in their own 48 cities.

Why choose the whole tribe of Levites? Maybe because they were few in numbers. According to the Book of Ezra, out of 42,360 returnees to Israel from Persia the Levites were not very numerous: "I reviewed the people and the priests, but I did not find any Levites there...Thanks to the benevolent care of our God for us, they brought us a capable man of the family of Mahli son of Levi son of Israel, and Sherebiah and his sons and brothers, 18 in all, and Hashabia, and with him Jeshaiah of the family of Merari, his brothers and their sons, 20 in all; and of the temple servants whom David and the officers had appointed for the service of the Levites – 220 temple servants, all of them listed by name." (Ezra 8:15, 18-20) After their return to the Land of Israel at the end of the 6th century BCE, the Levites immediately resumed their supervision of the newly restored Temple in Jerusalem. They were very important in teaching the Torah to the Jews who knew little about it.

Another more plausible reason for the selection of the Levites is that they were committed and maybe even hot tempered when it comes to the defense of family and faith. Remember that Levi and Simeon led the slaughter of the men of Shechem after the latter abused their sister. Remember that Moses, the Levite, killed an Egyptian who was abusing an Israelite slave. And, most important, after Moses discovered the golden calf (Ex 32:19) he shouted to everyone: "Who is on the Lord's side? Let him come to me. And all the Levites gathered themselves to him." (Ex 32:26-28) The Levites were loyal, and they destroyed the leaders of this revolt. In short, the Lord and Moses knew they could depend on the Levites to defend the Torah.

During the 2,000 years since the destruction of the Temple no one can claim with absolute certainty to know who is a Levite and who is not. The Talmud tells us that any Israelite who is pure according to the Levitical rules as explained in the Book of Leviticus can carry out the tasks of Levites. (Eiruvin 105a) I conclude that it is incumbent on all Jews to strive, as best we can, to reach toward the general principles and goals of purity and obedience to the commandments required of Levites and priests in this book. In that sense, the Book of Leviticus is as relevant for us today as it was for the Levites and priests over 2,000 years ago.

# 26

## Sh'mini

◆

### (Leviticus 9:1–11:47)

In Parashat *Tsav*, we read about the seven days of ordination or installation of the priests. In this Parashah we read what happened on the eighth day, *be yom hash'mini*. *Sh'mini*, eighth, is, of course, the name of the Parashah. On this day Aaron, the high priest, and the Israelites used the new altar for the first time by making sacrifices of animals and grains. Moses tells them about the significance of their actions: "For today the Lord will appear to you." (Lev 9:4)

We know that God's use of certain numbers follows a definite pattern. Forty tends to mean transformation, for example. This pattern is an important mnemonic device, no more than that. The number helps us remember the significance of certain well-defined actions. What, then, about the number eight? What does eight signify in Torah?

1. We have *Sh'mini Atzeret*, the eighth day of assembly at the end of the festival of *Sukkot*. According to *Zohar* ( *Zohar, Vayikra*, III:31b- 32a) "On the seventh day of Tabernacle, the judgment of the world is finally sealed and the edicts are sent forth from the king, and God's might is aroused...." [then] "on the next day (the Eighth Day of Assembly) they are to rejoice in [God] and to receive from Him blessings for all the year." We also start praying for rain that day.
2. Solomon's Temple was finished in the eighth month of the year. (I Kings 6:38)
3. Eight days are required for the Israelites to cleanse the Temple in both the eighth century BCE (II Chron 29:17) and later in the second century BCE which we commemorate with the eight day festival of Chanukah.
4. The most famous eight is the circumcision of all Jewish males exactly eight days after birth, even if the eighth day is the Sabbath. God

instructs Abraham: "You shall circumcise the flesh of your foreskin, and that shall be the sign of the covenant between Me and you. And throughout the generations, every male among you shall be circumcised at the age of eight days." (Gen 17:11 – 12) Immediately after the circumcision the father of the baby must say the following: "Blessed art thou, Lord our God...who has...commanded us to introduce my son into the covenant of Abraham our father."

These words, "introduce my son into the covenant," are the key for the understanding of the meaning of the number eight. The contract, the Covenant, has been signed, so to speak; it has been approved by all parties by this act of circumcision. On each of the eighth days or months - the rejoicing during *Sh'mini Atzeret* or assembly, the finishing of the Temple, the cleansing of the Temple, and circumcision – we affirm our relationship with God.

Put another way, the number eight reminds us that we are not passive observers; we act; we assert; we move; we defend. Studying this Parashah, *Sh'mini,* helps us reaffirm our eternal partnership with the Almighty

# 27

## *Tazri-a*

✦

## *(Leviticus 12:1-13:59)*

Parashat *Tazri-a,* focuses on ritual uncleanliness and the process of purification. Although most of the Parashah deals with the need for purification of persons suffering from a skin disease, the first eight verses refer to how a woman who has given birth purifies herself. In addition to a period of isolation, she must make an offering to expiate a sin. How could a woman who delivers a baby have sinned in any way? Some sages of the Talmud came up with an ironic explanation: during the pain and discomfort of giving birth the woman might have had bad thoughts about her husband and might have wished for no further relationship with him. Thus, she needs to expiate these thoughts.

Childbirth and female bodily functions were so important that a tractate of the Talmud- *Niddah* - is devoted to them. The word *niddah* has been translated as uncleanness, and much of the writing deals with the natural bodily functions of adult women. For example, they must be isolated for several days each month, and they must purify themselves. Rabbis of the Talmud gave a plausible reason for the need for isolation: "The Almighty wants the husband to stay away from his wife from time to time so that he will appreciate her more." (*Niddah* 31b) An important part of the tractate also deals with the natural bodily functions of adult men – some are polluting, and men must purify themselves before approaching the holy sanctuary.

Since the Temple no longer exists, one might assume that certain rules concerning uncleanliness and purity are irrelevant. On the contrary, whether we can follow them or not, these rules teach us about Judaism's direct and unashamed approach to the human body and the body's basic functions. For example, the idea that a baby could be born without the intimate interactions of a male and a female is foreign to the Torah and Judaism.

It is interesting to look at European painting from earliest times to see how one very rich and productive culture looks at childbirth and infants. For example, it seems that Spanish artists before modern times did not like to portray babies and children as they are. Except for idealized portraits of the baby Jesus, it seems that Spanish society found childbirth and babies and even small children to be rather disgusting. Children of art patrons and kings were, therefore, portrayed as if they were very clean and beautiful small adults – no runny noses, no dirty hands, no diapers to wash. The paintings are, of course, magnificent, but unrealistic.

There is no Jewish representational art of that period to compare, but from this Parashah and others we know that our holy texts are not limited to our spiritual lives; they deal with all aspects of our material and physical existence without any prudishness including the clean, the unclean, our bodies, our food, our clothes, our animals and land are in the Torah.

We make mistakes, but we can correct them and repent. We are supposed to do better next time. If we are physically or ritually unclean, the Almighty gives us ways to make ourselves clean again. What is the underlying message in the Book of Leviticus? The message is that the whole Torah is a book about living.

# 28

## *M'tzora*

✦

## *(Leviticus 14:1-15:33)*

Discussion of various forms of impurity and the ways to remove them, begun in the last Parashah, continues here although the subject has less resonance with most Jews today than most other subjects. It is a difficult subject, but I find the figurative applications interesting and relevant.

Possibly the worst form of impurity is *m'tzora,* a word which has been translated as "leper "and which is the name of the Parashah. According to the text, after the physical healing of the symptoms, which are a "scaly affliction," a priest goes through a very elaborate ceremony of purification.

The Almighty explains that once the Israelites arrive in the land of Canaan they may observe that their houses suffer from the same "scaly affliction." What is to be done about that? We read that the owner must inform a priest who inspects the walls: if there are green or red streaks, the house must be closed for seven days. After that period of time if the plague is still present, stones must be removed from the walls and thrown outside the city. The owner must scrape the walls and put in new stones and plaster. If the plague reappears, the house is basically impure, *temah.* Tear it down and build another house of different stones. This concept of a sick, polluted, infected house – here is where the figurative interpretation comes in.

Like the impurities affecting men and women and clothing, the meaning of a "leprous" house may be literal or figurative. Men and women have the bodily emissions we have read about; they may - albeit rarely - suffer from the terrible disease leprosy; although inanimate objects like clothing and the walls of houses do get moldy and may harbor diseases, a literal interpretation is difficult.

Rashi proposed one rather implausible literal explanation for the strange color of the infected house walls: he said that the earlier inhabitants of the houses, namely, the Amorites, fled before the Israelites arrived and hid their gold in the walls to prevent the Israelites from seizing it. The presence of the gold gradually changed the color of the walls, so when the priests ordered the removal of some stones or the demolition of the house, the Israelites could find the gold. (Rashi on Lev14:34) The distinguished 20th century French rabbi, Elie Munk, wrote that cleansing the houses was actually one way of ridding the land of the last vestiges of Canaanite presence (Munk, *The Call...Leviticus,* citing R. Shimon, p.152).

Two thousand years ago the sages considered the subject of the "leprous house" so important that they devoted a chapter of a tractate (treatise) of the rabbinic Mishnah to it. (Chapter 12 of *Negaim,*plagues) The most interesting comments are, however, found in the Tosefta, a rabbinic supplement to the Mishnah dating from about the year 300 of the Common Era. The sages quoted in the Tosefta deny the possibility of a literal interpretation saying "A diseased house has never come into existence and is never going to come into existence." (Neusner, citing *Negaim,* 6:1A, p. 1730)

According to the rabbinic commentary in the Tosefta, what we call plagues are a result of disputes which create cracks and eruptions in a community. Hirsch expands this idea to say that a house becomes "sick", so to speak, when its inhabitants have behaved in selfish ways. (*Hirsch*, p. 394) Selfishness is by definition anti-social. Munk continues that any signs of breakdown in the structure of a house, presumably inhabited by several people, may reflect a wider breakdown in society. Reform and maybe more basic changes are needed.

This Parashah is read and studied as the festival of Passover is approaching. Jews are busy cleaning their houses to remove any traces of *chametz* or leavening as a sign of solidarity with the Jews who fled from Egypt without leavening for bread. A literal search for the pollution of leavening can correspond with the more figurative search for breaches in the walls and other structures, both visible and invisible, which define families and communities. Even though there are no priests to help in the search and cure, the Almighty has faith in humans' ability to understand the symptoms of illness and to try to eliminate the causes.

# 29

## *Acharei Mot*

✦

## *(Leviticus 16:1 – 18:30)*

Two of Aaron's sons, Nadav and Abihu, were killed by God, according to the text in Parashat *Sh'mini*, because they made a serious mistake during a ceremony at the sanctuary. The text says that they approached the altar where "they offered before the Lord alien fire, which He had not enjoined upon them." (Lev 10: 1-2) God kills these two men. The narrative after this shocking event is suspended in the subsequent two Parashot, *Tazri-a* and *M'tzora*.

This Parashah, *Acharei Mot*, which means "after the death" of Aaron's sons, picks up the narrative again with various instructions to Aaron in his role as high priest as if practically nothing had happened. Neither Aaron nor Moses is allowed to dwell on these events, and Aaron is instructed to fulfill certain specific duties during Yom Kippur. For example: as High Priest he must enter the Holy of Holies to "make expiation for himself and his household and for the whole congregation of Israel." (Lev16:17). Then he places his hands on the head of a goat thereby transmitting the sins of Israel onto the goat. We also read some additions to the laws of *kashrut* such as the interdiction against consuming the blood of animals we have slaughtered for food.

For me the most interesting part of this Parashah is: "You shall not copy the practices of the Land of Egypt where you dwelled or of the Land of Canaan to which I am taking you, nor shall you follow their laws." (Lev 18:3) Why is the Almighty worried that the Israelites will copy these two peoples?

Remember that the Israelites were desert nomads and that both the Egyptians and the Canaanites were among the great urban civilizations of antiquity. Canaanites and their Phoenician cousins to the north built impressive city-states throughout the Mediterranean Sea including Carthage and Marseilles. They were great traders and artisans whose buildings, ships,

85

public works projects and art could amaze the nomads, and the latter might be tempted to copy them. They might also be tempted to copy Canaanite idol worship and associated sexual practices which were very different from what God commanded and forbade. Not surprisingly, God taught the Israelites to drive out all the Canaanites from the Promised Land.

Here is a paradox: despite the order to drive the Canaanites out of the Promised Land, they do not disappear from the Bible. Israelites continue to interact with them. Most significantly, the half shekel used to pay the annual Temple tax was minted in Tyre, a Phoenician city, and an image of the Canaanite god Melkart figured on that coin. Jews depended on and copied other neighbors in many ways. From about the 6th century BCE Jews gave up the Hebrew script and wrote the Torah with Aramaic letters.

In short, despite the admonition to avoid mixing with the other nations and to avoid copying them in order to remain exclusive, Jews have never been able to maintain complete separation from others and their surroundings. Jews survive as a people among other peoples by striking a delicate balance between the evolving culture of secular daily life and living according to the laws, *halakhah*. *Halakhah* is our ideal. We follow it imperfectly. God, who understands and forgives our weaknesses if we repent, has not struck us down. Despite our failures, we have survived while the more powerful nations of antiquity have not.

# 30

## *K'doshim*

✦

## *(Leviticus 19:1-20:27)*

In this Parashah God instructs Moses to tell the "whole Israelite community...
You shall be holy." - *K'doshim*, the name of the Parashah. In order to fulfill
this order the Israelites must obey the commandments which are once again
listed. Because of this repetition and the emphasis on "emulating God's
intrinsic holiness," scholars "designate the textual unit from chapter 17
through chapter 26 as the Holiness Code." (Alter, 625, ftn 2)

One might wonder why everything, particularly the commandments, is
repeated so frequently in the Torah. Didn't we hear the commandments at
Mount Sinai already?

The reasons for repetition are first, Torah is a written account of oral
messages. God speaks to Moses, and Moses speaks to the children of Israel.
Speaking style is repetitious to help people understand the basic points.
Second, our ancestors needed reminders of God's commandments because
they were forgetful and disobedient. Later generations were not physically
present at Sinai.

The third reason is that there are subtle and important differences each
time a command is repeated. To understand them we need the biblical scholars.
For example, at the beginning of the text this week we read: "Speak to the
whole Israelite community" rather than the customary "speak to the children
of Israel." Ramban explains: "Our Rabbis have already said that this section
was addressed to the full assembly [of all Israel]" (Ramban on Lev 19:2) In an
explanatory note, the editor of Ramban's text wrote that according to Rabbi
Elijah Mizrachi (circa 1455-1526) commenting on Rashi, "[s]ince these laws
are so fundamental, men, women, and children were all present when Moses
addressed them, whereas in the other sections of the Torah only the elders and
the men were present." (*Ramban*,on Leviticus 19:2, ftn 2) This means women

and children also have responsibility for fulfilling the duties imposed by the commandments. In other words, the commandments are inclusive.

A fourth reason is that repetition permits amplification, explanation or summary; it is an excellent didactic device. There are many commandments concerning our relations with other persons, such as the interdiction against coveting one's neighbor's possessions. For the first time, however, we read in this Parashah: "And you shall love your neighbor as yourself." (Lev 19:18) This statement has been called the "Golden Rule" and, at first glance, it sounds perfect as an ethical guide. Is it possible?

Ramban says it is not realistic that we can literally love someone – particularly someone not related to us – as we love ourselves. (Ramban on Lev 19:18) More realistically, Ramban says that the statement means: don't be jealous of others and do the good things for your neighbor that you wish for yourself. The great Hillel put the Golden Rule another way: "What is hateful to you, do not do to your neighbor." The commandments concerning relations with others are basically the same, but the new formulation gives us a deeper understanding.

Put another way, through the study and comparison of the commandments in Torah we should be able to reach new heights in our efforts to understand the Almighty's messages in our own times. We were not present at Sinai, but our holy texts can speak to us – men, women, and children – as if we were there. We too can try to become holy - *K'doshim.*

# 31

## *Emor*

✦

## *(Leviticus 21:1-24:23)*

In Parashat *Emor* we read the following: "There came out from among the Israelites one whose mother was Israelite and whose father was Egyptian. And a fight broke out in the camp between that half-Israelite and a certain Israelite. The son of the Israelite woman pronounced the Name in blasphemy, and he was brought to Moses – now his mother's name was Shlomith daughter of Devree of the tribe of Dan….And the Lord spoke to Moses saying: Take the blasphemer outside the camp, and let all who were within hearing lay their hands upon his head, and let the whole community stone him." (Lev 24:11-14)

Then God sets a general rule for future behavior: "Anyone who blasphemes his God shall bear his guilt; if he also pronounced the name Lord, he shall be put to death. The whole community shall stone him, stranger or citizen, if he has thus pronounced the Name, he shall be put to death." (Lev 24:15-16) This is a story about blasphemy. What can blasphemy mean for us today?

Blasphemy is a form of cursing. In general, cursing verbally degrades someone or something. It can be rather mundane such as in Proverbs 11:26: "He that withholds grain, the people will curse him…." Calling on occult powers to injure someone is more serious. In the Book of Numbers (Num 22:4-24:25) we read that Balak hires Balaam to curse the Israelites so that Balak "can thus defeat them and drive them out of the land." (Num 22:6) Cursing can have fatal consequences for the person who uses it: "He who reviles his father or his mother shall be put to death." (Exodus 21:17) The most potent and dangerous form of cursing is blasphemy which defames the deity, maliciously reviles God, negates the Almighty. (Leonard Levy, pp. 3, 45)

In Judaism blasphemy is very narrowly defined; according to Talmud, it is uttering "the ineffable Name." meaning, of course, the Tetragrammaton.

(Sanhedrin 56a) The blasphemer in this Parashah is stoned to death for pronouncing as well as cursing the Name.

What do we know about the blasphemer from the narrative in Leviticus and from the Talmud, Midrash and Zohar? He has a complicated biography with an old, indirect connection with Moses. His mother is called Shlomith, and she is the daughter of a man called Devree from the tribe of Dan. Midrash tells us that the Egyptian taskmaster that the young Moses killed (because the taskmaster was beating an Israelite slave) was the father of the blasphemer. The Egyptian was beating the Israelite because the latter was the husband of Shlomith with whom the Egyptian had an intimate relationship. When the Israelite discovered the relationship, the Egyptian wanted to kill him. (*Midrash Rabbah Leviticus*, XXXII:4)

In due course Shlomith gives birth to her and the Egyptian's son. He is, of course, a *mamzer*, the offspring of a forbidden relationship because his mother is already married. This means he cannot marry a "legitimate Jew", and he is subject to certain humiliations. He might have been better off staying in Egypt, but he chooses to accompany the Israelites when they depart for the Promised Land.

Because his mother and grandfather are Danites, the blasphemer wants to travel and to live among this tribe. They reject him because patrilineal descent determines tribal identity, and people seem to know that his father was an Egyptian. Midrash explains that this exclusion is the reason for his anger. Midrash also tells us "He appealed to the court of Moses to be admitted into the tribe of Dan and lost his case...." (*Midrash Rabbah-Leviticus*, XXXII:3) He realizes he has no identity, except for *mamzer*.

After the failed appeal to Moses he begins to argue and to fight with another man who, according to Zohar, "insulted [his] mother" and told him that his Egyptian father had been killed by Moses. (Zohar *Vayikra*, 3:106a) In a state of high rage he curses with the Holy Name. After that outburst he was brought before Moses who ordered that he be stoned to death.

The blasphemer was weaker than Job who resisted the temptation to curse the Almighty. Job is being tortured by Satan in order to test his faith. He has lost his children and his possessions and then suffers a painful inflammation of his whole body. His wife advises him that if he blasphemes, he will die and thus be released from the suffering. Job rejects the suggestion saying: "Should we accept only good from God and not accept evil?" (Job 2:10) What are the lessons for modern Jews?

We are told that Jews are a holy people: "When Israel went forth from Egypt, the house of Jacob from a people of strange speech, Judah became His 'holy one,' Israel, His dominion." (Psalm 114: 1-2). Other peoples and individuals may reject this idea of Jews as a holy people, and they may curse and oppress Jews from time to time. Throughout most of our history we have not been able to do much about such verbal abuse. The problem is when Jews curse and revile each other because of their differing beliefs, backgrounds and behaviors in both the secular and religious realms. It is something we can do something about.

Even if we do not wake up each morning with the thought that we are part of a holy people, we can try to think of other individual Jews as holy – including those who are different from us. With that idea in mind we should never allow ourselves to revile other Jews. Reviling and cursing others will lead to self-destruction. Jewish survival as one people depends on our ability to seek ways to respect one another.

# 32

## B'har

✦

## (Leviticus 25:1-26:2)

The opening words in this Parashah are "The Lord spoke to Moses on Mount [B'har] Sinai." The Lord is reminding us that all our laws originate from the Theophany, God's revelation to Moses, on Mount Sinai. Thus, even though the specific commandments in this Parashah are not to be found in Parashat *Yitro* in the Book of Exodus, we believe they are part of that message from the Almighty, as Rashi explains. (Rashi on Lev 25:1)

For example, the Lord gives very specific commandments about the cultivation of the land of Israel subsequent to Israelite settlement there. After six years of cultivation Israelites must observe a "sabbath of complete rest" for the land (Lev 25:4) Sowing and reaping are forbidden, but the Israelites may eat what trees and plants naturally produce. The year after seven Sabbaticals (the fiftieth year according to most authorities) is supposed to be observed as a "Jubilee Year." During this 50th year there will be no sowing or reaping as in the case of any sabbatical year. In addition, people will return to land they lost as a result of loans; land and homes previously sold will be redeemed; servants and slaves are to be freed.

With respect to slaves, there were also very specific instructions. The late Dr. Ephraim Urbach, a highly respected professor of Talmud at Hebrew University, dealt with them in detail. (See Brody and Herr) There were rules about treatment of non-Jewish and Jewish slaves.

What Jews became slaves to other Jews? There were two categories of Jewish slaves:

1. Thieves and other criminals paid for that which they had stolen by working for the people they had wronged;

2.   The desperately poor who could not feed their families. During the period of the Talmud, wealthy Babylonian rabbis obtained Jewish slaves by paying government taxes for them. (Brody, pp. 69, 143)

It is also written in this Parashah that Jews have an obligation to redeem Jewish slaves held by non-Jews living in Israel. (Lev. 25:47-49) Ironically, the redeemed Jews promptly went to work as slaves for their fellow Jews, but they could be slaves only for a maximum of seven years. They could refuse to be freed after the seven years elapsed, and there was a special ceremony indicating their acquiescence. "Until the time of the Maccabees, it was Jewish slaves who supplied the principal labour force for the property-owning class and the large estates." (Brody, p. 70) Jews also owned non-Jewish slaves, whom they called Canaanites; they endeavored to convert these men and women until the 4th century CE when the very anti-Jewish emperor, Constantine, forbade Jewish ownership of non-Jewish slaves.

Many rabbinical rulings regulate the treatment of slaves, their manumission, and sale. The loss of an arm, a leg, an eye, and even a tooth were grounds for automatic manumission. Like the *get*, the written form given by a husband to his wife in a divorce, the owner had to give the freed slave a formal certificate.

The Talmud says owners had to give the slaves the same food and housing as themselves. Owners were forbidden to sell Jewish slaves outside Israel, but in fact Jews were sold to foreigners in Syria because of economic necessity. (Brody, pp. 126-127) As much as we might hope for it, never, according to Professor Urbach, did the rabbis of Talmud condemn slavery on moral or ethical grounds. Like other societies of the times, "slavery was taken for granted." (Brody, p. 59)

Professor Urbach says, slavery was part of the social reality in Israel from about the 6th century BCE through the fourth century CE. (Brody, pp. 50-156), but it disappeared from Israel. We study these and all other aspects of our past even though some chapters are a bit unsettling to the modern mind. In recent history Jews have been at the forefront of movements struggling for human equality and justice, but trafficking in women (including to Israel), growing inequalities in income and in quality of life mean there is no reason to feel complacent about our world.

# 33

## *B'chukkotai*

✦

### *(Leviticus 26:3-27:34)*

In this Torah reading God shows His confidence that Israel will do what is necessary to maintain the structures and personnel of the religious institutions that God has established. The theme of this short Parashah is, therefore, how and why money is given to the mobile sanctuary which the Israelites built before reaching the Promised Land. Later generations, who built the permanent Temple in Jerusalem, were to be guided by these instructions concerning the temporary structure of the mobile sanctuary.

Gedaliah Alon, one of the foremost historians of rabbinic Judaism, asserted that the Temple, the *Beit ha-Mikdash,* which contained the Holy Ark, was a critical part of Jewish life even after Jews had already developed other places for prayer and study. (Alon, pp. 46-49) He said that the Temple served as:

1. The only site where the entire nation could worship as a nation.
2. [T]he only place for the atonement of sins through sacrifice
3. "[T]he focus of the great religious events in the life of the nation" such as Pesach which is "central to the identity and solidarity of all Jews worldwide."
4. The Temple and surrounding area were a "public forum for the dissemination of ideas"
5. Within the Temple resided the Divine Presence or *Shekhinah* which was "the center and focus of all that was bound up in the faith in Israel's God."

Money in the form of silver paid for the maintenance of the Temple and its personnel, the Levites and Kohanim. The Levites and Kohanim took food from the sacrifices of animals, grains and fruit, but they also needed silver for the Temple structures – Temple utensils had to be replaced; artisans had to be paid, and, according to the Mishnah in Tractate Shekalim of the Jerusalem Talmud, funds from the the Temple treasury also paid for the maintenance of the walls, towers and water supply of the city of Jerusalem. The mandatory annual tax of ½ shekel paid by each male 20 years and older had proven inadequate.

Chapter 27 of Leviticus suggests other sources of income. A person could contribute by vowing the value of a human being. Instead of dedicating the service of a person to God, as Hanna dedicated the service of her son Samuel, one could contribute money. The amount of silver was 50 shekel weight for a male 20 to 60 years of age. (Lev 27:3) For those too poor to pay this sum, the priest could arrange a lesser amount. Animals could be donated to the Temple, and the priests would appraise them. The donor would then redeem the animal with silver at the appraised value plus 20%.

In addition, one-tenth – a tithe – of one's herds was to be given to the Temple. It could be redeemed by the owner for the value plus 20%. Lastly, if owners of houses and land wished to "consecrate" their property, they would obtain an appraisal from the priests. In the Book of Numbers, 18:8, the Lord speaks directly to Aaron about receiving the donations mentioned in Leviticus 27. The Lord also adds another source of funds, namely the five shekels that parents must give for the redemption of the first born.

What do we know about the actual payments by the Israelites? Did they really donate to the Temple? One answer comes from the prophet Malachi. He complained that the Israelites were not paying enough to the Temple: "Ought man to defraud God? Yet you are defrauding Me…. Bring the full tithe into the storehouse…." (Mal 3:8-10)

Evidence from the prophets and from Luke in the Christian Bible (Luke 11:42) indicates that both secular and religious authorities were unrelenting in their pursuit of donations and tithes. They may have expected too much of the people. According to Schuerer's history of the Jews, "Great wealth must finally have flowed into the Temple…. In the Temple treasury were thirteen trumpet-shaped coffers into which money intended for particular liturgical purposes was dropped. No fewer than six of these contained 'voluntary gifts' pure and simple." (Schuerer, p.274) The sages of Mishnah and Talmud as well as Maimonides wrote extensively about the proper form of donation and tithing.

Year in and year out the Jews paid even though many lived far from Jerusalem. They continued to pay even after the destruction of the Temple, meaning no one could force them to do so. Money went to the Patriarch or *Nasi* in the Galilee whom the Roman authorities recognized as the leader of the Jews within their empire. Later the Jews sent contributions to the academies in Babylon and other Jewish institutions.

God seemed to sense the willingness of Jews to contribute to the mobile sanctuary and then to the Temple in Jerusalem. God issued no threat. In Leviticus chapter 27 God depended on voluntarism. Imperfectly but consistently we have done what God expected us to do.

This voluntarism which continued after the destruction of the Temple has helped Jews survive for 2,000 years without central religious or political authority. It has eased the trauma and the transition from state and Temple to Diaspora communities and synagogues and community center and schools which we sustain and which sustain us today.

# B'MIDBAR/NUMBERS

# 34

## B'midbar

✦

## (Numbers 1:1 – 4:20)

We begin reading the fourth book of Torah, Numbers or *B'midbar*. This book seems to be the most time-bound book of Torah because, as Ramban explained, it deals with the journey in the desert – *b'midbar*. "There are no commandments in this book which are binding for all times except for some commandments about the [Temple] offerings...." (Ramban on *Numbers*, "Introduction," p. 4) However, it seems to me that everything in the Torah has some application over space and over time. For example, we have much to learn from this book about the census, enemies both internal and external, and about other issues.

The Lord prepares the Israelites militarily for the hazardous crossing of the land between Egypt and the Promised Land. A census is necessary in order to organize a proper fighting force, and the Almighty instructs Moses to count all males twenty and older according to tribe. God chooses men from each tribe to assist Moses; they will be both military leaders and the elected of what the text called "the assembly." (Num 1:16, Cf. Excursus 1 by Milgrom, pp. 335-336)

Let us examine the census, an important function of state leadership, but fraught with controversy from ancient times to the present. We read in the Torah that only God has the right to order a census. Even then, a census must be taken with great care. In the Book of Exodus, the first census is done only indirectly through the collection of the half-shekel: the half-shekel given by every male 20 and older is counted, not the human beings themselves. This particular census had a religious purpose as well since the money collected went to pay the expenses of building the Sanctuary in the desert.

When Jewish rulers took the initiative to order a census, God became angry. For example, King David ordered a census, and the text says: "Satan arose against Israel and incited David to number Israel." (I Chron 21:1) God subsequently punished the king. The account in II Samuel, chapter 24 is different; it seems that God instructed David to take a census. Nonetheless, "David reproached himself for having numbered the people." (II Samuel 24:10)

What is the problem with a human-initiated census? According to Ramban, "God does not want all Israel to be limited by numbers since He will multiply them like the stars of heaven...." (Ramban on Num 1:3) The Prophet Hosea says: "The number of the people of Israel shall be like that of the sands of the sea, which cannot be measured or counted...." (Hosea 2:1) If the Israelites take a census on their own initiative, it might imply that they do not sufficiently trust God.

When non-Jews take a census of Jews, Jews have feared the tax consequences, and they may have been convinced that the rulers were about to take some initiative against Jewish laws and practices. For example, in the year 6 CE, the Roman governor of Syria, to which Israel was attached, ordered a census which led the Jews to revolt. (Gabba, pp. 132-133) In modern times the Nazis famously used censuses in their genocidal efforts against Jews.

Since World War II Jews in the Diaspora and in Israel have conducted meticulous calculations of the Jewish population. Isn't this against the will of God?

With the loss of one-third of the Jewish people in the *Shoa*/Holocaust and the threat of assimilation, leaders of Jewish communities say they must know about Jewish population trends for survival. Survival in the wilderness – *b'midbar* – of Sinai depended on counting and organizing potential soldiers as we read in this Parashah; survival in the Diaspora today depends, for example, on counting Jewish children and organizing educational programs for them.

We adapt to the exigencies of our times. We must take measures, including censuses, in order to ensure our survival and strength.

# 35

## *Naso*

✦

## *(Numbers 4:21-7:89)*

In this second Parashah of the Book of Numbers Moses continues to take
– *Naso*, the name of the Parashah – the census, particularly with respect to
the Levites. We learn the details of Levite service at the Sanctuary. Next
we read rules concerning punishment for fraud, and regulations for taking
a Nazarite vow (of abstinence). We learn the priestly blessing, and we learn
rules concerning an ordeal to test a wife suspected of adultery.

The details of this ordeal are painfully clear: the husband brings her
to the priest with a grain offering. The priest uncovers her head in public –
considered to be very humiliating; he then prepares a mixture of holy water,
ink used for writing curses and some earth from the floor of the Tabernacle;
he makes her drink the mixture. If she is innocent, the text tells us, nothing
will happen to her, but if she is guilty, she will suffer great pain and will be
sterile for life. The last verse protects the husband from punishment even if
his suspicions are false.

In other words, a man has nothing to lose by accusing his wife of infidelity.
She, on the other hand, is publicly humiliated even if she is innocent. This
seems cruel and unfair, and in the First Century of the Common Era the
influential and courageous leader, Rabbi Yohanan Ben Zakkai, took action.

A word about this important person: In the year 68 CE Rabbi Yohanan
fled Jerusalem which the Romans had under siege. He settled in the town of
Yavneh on the coast of Israel along with his students and other rabbis. There
he established an academy for the study of Jewish texts and traditions; he set
up a court, which among other things maintained a standard calendar for all
Jews. (Cf. Neusner, 1970)

After the destruction of the Temple in the year 70 he decreed that certain
rituals that previously took place only in the Temple would henceforth take
place in all synagogues such as waving the *lulav* on Sukkot and the priestly

blessing that we read in this Parashah. In other words, Rabbi Yohanan ensured continuity after the destruction of the Temple and the Jewish state. He also made changes including the abolition of the ordeal of the suspected adulteress. He understood the unfairness of it saying that husbands had to prove that they themselves were innocent of adultery before daring to accuse their wives. Because proving a negative is difficult, husbands could in practice never make accusations against their wives.

Rabbi Yohanan ben Zakkai explained how Jews survive through the millennia – keeping the essentials of the Covenant while adapting to the times and environment. Countries have mottos expressing their essential values, such as the American E Pluribus Unum and the French Liberty, Equality and Fraternity. Based on our own history and experience, one Jewish motto should be Continuity and Change.

# 36

## *B'ha-alot'kha*

✦

### *(Numbers 8:1 – 12:16)*

In this Parashah, the Almighty instructs the priests to set up and light – *B'ha-alot'kha* the name of the Parashah – the seven-branched lamps at the sanctuary. Then, God explains the special role of the Levites: "Thus you shall set the Levites apart from the Israelites, and the Levites shall be Mine." (Num 8:6-20) Henceforth, they shall serve in the sanctuary in place of the first born who were saved when God killed all the Egyptian firstborn. Rashi explains that God had originally planned that the firstborn of all the tribes would serve Him, but since they sinned by worshipping the golden calf, they are excluded: "And I have taken the Levites instead of all the firstborn of the people of Israel." (Num 8:18, 44)

After the construction of the sanctuary, the job of the Levites, from the age of 25 to the age of 50, was to care for the structure and the ceremonial implements used in the sanctuary. For the first five years of their service they must study, and then at the age of 30 they are ready to carry the mobile sanctuary and are qualified to sing and to assist the priests. (Num 8:24-25) Because of these tasks, the Levites were not given a portion of the land in Israel to tend. The other tribes must take care of the material needs of the Levites.

Why did the Almighty choose the Levites for the honor of Temple service? Remember that their ancestor, Levi, the son of Jacob and Leah, was short-tempered. He killed the men who abducted his sister Dinah (Genesis 34:25) and paid no attention to his exasperated father's criticism. When Levi knew what he had to do in order to protect the family, he did it. Jacob always remembered Levi's actions, and at the end of his life Jacob's parting words are harsh. He curses Levi's anger and says others should be aware of his hot-tempered nature. (Genesis 49:5) Jacob is worried about Levi's apparent zealousness. Levi's descendant, Moses, shows the same anger when he sees an Egyptian overseer beating an Israelite slave. Without thinking twice about the possible terrible consequences of defending a slave, Moses strikes and kills the Egyptian. As a result of this action, Moses flees the life of comfort he had enjoyed in the court of the Egyptian king. This loyalty to his people and this willingness to sacrifice so much may be one reason God chose Moses to lead the Israelites out of Egypt.

After the exodus from Egypt, the Levites, the least numerous of the tribes, were the most loyal to Moses; they rallied quickly and without hesitation to Moses' side once he destroyed the golden calf. It is conceivable that otherwise there might have been a general revolt, but Moses shouted "Who is on the Lord's side? Let him come to me. And all the Levites gathered themselves together to him." (Exodus 32:26) They quickly killed 3,000 rebellious Israelites.

Ramban says that the Levites had not participated in the worship of the golden calf; instead they warned their fellow Israelites against the temptation to idolatry. Moreover, the Levites knew who the guilty persons were, and they dispatched them by the sword. (Ramban on Ex 32:27) Thus, we are to conclude that God knows He can count on Levite intelligence, resolve and loyalty. Their emotions were honest, and they channeled their energy to serve the people and God.

We all can serve God with our deeds and our intellect, irrespective of ethnic, social, gender or other identities. Levi and his descendants show that we also serve the Almighty with our emotion and our passions as long as they are carefully focused on protection of the community and fulfillment of the commandments.

# 37

## Sh'lach L'kha

✦

## (Numbers 13:1-15:41)

Twice a day we read God's instructions in the third paragraph of the *Sh'ma* to look at the *tsitsit*, the fringes on our *tallit* or prayer shawl, in order to remember the commandments. The words come from verses in Parsahat *Sh'lach L'kha* (Num. 15:37-41) According to the English text of all prayer books, God tells us that remembering the commandments will protect us from being led astray or seduced by the desires of our hearts and eyes. The key phrase is *atem zonim acharechem* (Num 15:39) The Jewish Publication Society translation of this phrase is that by looking at the fringe you can remember and obey the commandments "so that you do not follow your heart and eyes in your lustful urge." In this context, the word *zonim* seems to mean lustful urge for false gods. Its root, *zayin-nun-hei*, also forms the noun "prostitute," and the verb "to commit fornication." (Schaechter-Haham, pp. 175-176)

According to a recent book, lust is "the enthusiastic desire, the desire that infuses the body, for sexual activity and its pleasures for their own sake," (Blackburn, p. 19). Lust begins by looking at or imagining someone or something. Rashi comments about this idea (Rashi on Numbers 15:39) "The heart and the eyes are the 'spies' of the body – they act as its agents for sinning. The eye sees; the heart covets; and the body commits the sin." (Rashi on Numbers 15:39, and he is referring to the Jerusalem Talmud Ber I:8, Tanch)

We associate wearing *tsitsit* with prayers, but Ibn Ezra suggests that wearing and keeping our eyes on *tsitsit* protect us in the market place where a Jewish person may be tempted into sin by looking at other people and things. (*The Secret*, p. 124, ftn 77) Originally, Jews wore a square toga-like garment that had *tsitsit* for their daily secular activities. After people no longer wore such an external garment on a daily basis the *tallit* and *tsitsit* became a garment worn during prayer.

## What is the "evil inclination?"

For the rabbis of the Talmud lust is one manifestation of a deeper and more dangerous and palpable entity within the human spirit, which they have labeled the evil inclination, the *yetser ha-ra*. It is "energy within man's nature which, if left unchecked, moves him irrationally to sin." (Cohen Stuart, p. 49) In addition to lust, the evil inclination is a source of greed, selfishness, anger, jealousy. Some rabbis also personify *yetser ha-ra* as Satan.

Without the protection of the fringes (*tsitsit*), Seforno says, our urges "would eventually diminish the influence of [our] mind over [our] body to such an extent that it would lead to [our] premature death both in this world and in the hereafter." (Seforno on Num 15:39, cited in *Hachut Hameshulash*, Vol. 6, p. 1395) Submission to the evil inclination means that "no place is left for God and his Law, no room for thoughts of God as the Director of our actions and of our fate....." Logically, therefore, the ultimate sin toward which the evil inclination leads us is idolatry. What is the reason? The texts say: 'There shall be no strange god in thee, neither shall thou bow down to an alien god (Psalm 81:10). 'The stranger who is within you, you shall not make sovereign over you.'" (cited by Cohen Stuart, p. 49) In other words, by following our urges and impulses we might abandon those things which are really important to us, namely, life itself and the Almighty.

Two questions occur to me: How do we eliminate the evil inclination? How do we conquer the guilt we feel because of our awareness of the evil inclination within us? I shall propose answers after discussing the nature of the evil inclination.

In Torah there is no specific reference to the evil inclination although after the flood, God realizes that humanity is innately imperfect and says "the inclination of man's heart is evil from [the time of] his youth." (Gen 8:21) On the basis of this text from Genesis 8:21 the rabbis developed the concept. For example, in the view of Rashi, *yetser ha-ra* is a concept and entity; he says that "from the moment the embryo bestirs itself to have an independent existence the evil inclination is given to it." He refers to it six times in his commentary on the Torah and 41 times in his commentary on the Talmud. Rashi blames Adam: when he ate from the tree, the evil inclination "became an active principle in him." It "entered into him" (Rashi's commentary on Gen 2:25). He and other rabbis have expanded the concept and concluded that all humans down to the present day have inherited the evil inclination from Adam and Eve.

# How do we defeat the evil inclination?

The rabbinic answers included suppressing sexual feelings, studying Torah and praying.

First, Jews must not engage in the illicit sexual relationships which God lists in Leviticus 18: 6-23. The explicit reason is that they are the practices of the Canaanites. If Israel copies them, Israel will lose its own separateness and holiness. God tells us "Do not defile yourselves in any of those ways, for it is by such that the nations that I am casting out before you defiled themselves." (Lev 18:24) The implicit reason for forbidding these practices is the fear they will lead us to idolatry. For the Canaanites and their neighbors sex was an integral part of idol worship, and, therefore, copying their sexual practices might lead Israel to violate the first commandment, "You shall have no other gods besides Me." (Ex 20:3)

The Israelites almost succumbed at Baal-Peor. Remember that Balaam in Parashat *Balak* was unsuccessful in his efforts to curse the Israelites directly; as he departed he probably encouraged Moabite women to seduce Israelites with the promise of sex but really for idol worship. The exact words of the text are: "While Israel was staying at Shittim the people profaned themselves by whoring [the word is *zonim*] with the Moabite women, who invited the people to the sacrifices for their god." (Num 25:1-2) Therefore, the main contribution of Pinchas, who killed an Israelite man and a Moabite woman in the midst of their intimate embrace before the idol, was to bring an abrupt halt to Israelite idolatry. (Num 25:6-8)

Second, some rabbis have urged that Jews minimize even the acceptable forms of sex in their lives. Put another way: procreation yes; recreation no. Maimonides makes the strongest statements against sex. In his view all sexual relations should be "abhorred except for necessity" by which he means procreation. (Maimonides, III:49, p. 609)

Maimonides' asceticism is closer to Augustine than it is to mainstream Judaism.

Augustine told his fellow Christians that satisfying physical desires within marriage was a sin but "pardonable." (Biale, p. 98) The 1532 penal code of the Holy Roman Empire strictly prohibited non-procreative sex, and using contraceptive devices was punishable with death. (Blackburn, p.125) Mahatma Gandhi preached severe limitations on sexual relations and became celibate himself at a relatively young age. It is useful to remember, however, that no matter what holy texts and scholars say; no matter what laws proscribe, the masses of people of all religious communities maintain their own sexual practices which may or may not conform to the elites' views.

Despite the importance of Maimonides to Judaism, his asceticism is not a dominant current in Jewish thought. David Biale says that our tradition is actually more complex and Jewish texts are more ambivalent than Maimonides. *The Song of Songs*, which "explores the tension between desire and fulfillment," is without any doubt an "affirmation of eroticism." (Biale, pp. 31-32) We read many examples of romantic love, seduction, lust in our holy texts. Isaac falls in love with Rebecca; Jacob loves Rachel and Ruth seduces Boaz; and the romantic adventures of Kings David and Solomon are examples of erotic motivations. Judah's lust for Tamar, his daughter-in-law, ensures the proliferation of the tribe of Judah.

Thirdly, some of the rabbis have believed that the study of holy texts and frequent prayer can suppress the urge for sex. The great scholar Ephraim Urbach writes about these beliefs, namely, that the Torah is the antidote to the evil inclination. "Thus, despite everything, he who has been created wicked can be made righteous by virtue of the Torah which enables him to control his inclination." (Urbach, *The Sages*, pp. 282-283) Males receive much advice in the Talmud about what to do if their thoughts stray toward sex. One is to go immediately to the study house and immerse oneself in the study of the Torah.

The Chasidim (or Hasidim) accepted the human's physical urges although, according to Biale, the Baal Shem Tov, (Rabbi Israel ben Eliezer 1698-1760), a founder of the Chasidic movement saw physical pleasure as only a"stepping stone to the spiritual."(Biale, p. 131)  He is alleged to have said that "prayer is a form of intercourse with the *Shekhinah* (Holy Spirit)…" (*Tzavaat ha-Ribash*, no.68, p.21, cited in Biale, p.144) According to Biale, "Hasidism made God the object of desire for the purpose of constructing a community of ecstatic worshippers." (Biale, p.145) They tried to displace "sexuality from the human to the divine realm." (Biale, p.145)

Through prayer and study the devout say they are trying to develop a "good inclination" to challenge and defeat the bad inclination. According to midrash, a mature human being has both an inclination for good and an inclination for evil. (*Midrash Rabbah Genesis* XIV: 4, p. 114) Some rabbis from ancient times say that the good inclination comes into the male body at the age of 13. (Cohen Stuart,p. 15) Whether or not there is an entity called the *yetser ha tov*, at the beginning of adulthood, individuals can study Torah to counteract the evil inclination. Thus, the force for evil will not disappear from the body, but its manifestation can be suppressed and its energies redirected, sublimated.

The rabbis insist Jews should not strive to eliminate the evil inclination from our bodies and mind because they say we need it. "Nahman said in R. Samuel's name: 'But for the Evil Desire…no man would build a house, take

a wife and beget children...'" (Quoting from *Midrash Rabbah Genesis* IX:7)
What does this mean?

## The inclination without the evil?

The evil inclination – in our bodies from birth – precedes the good inclination
which we are told we can receive when we become bar and bat mitzvah. But,
preceding both the good and the evil inclination is simply the *yetser*. In the
texts I have mentioned, this word is translated as "inclination," a very bland
rendering. The origins of the meaning of this word can be found at the very
beginning of the Torah. In Genesis we read it is the verb describing how
God created Adam and Eve: "the Lord God formed man from the dust of
the earth." (Gen 2:7) The meaning of *yetser* in this context is "formed." The
Torah repeats the word *yetser* in the next verse when explaining that He put
Adam "whom he had formed" – into the Garden of Eden (Gen 2:8) Later,
the Prophet Isaiah refers to the work of the potter who forms – *yetser* - a
vessel out of clay. In his dictionary of the Talmud Jastrow expands the word
to mean the shaping and forming of thoughts. (Jastrow, p. 590)

It is legitimate to extend *yetser* further to mean "creative force." Thus, a
person under the total control of *yetser ha ra* is a solipsist, one whose creative
force is directed completely and solely toward self satisfaction without regard
to God, Torah, and other human beings. Succinctly, it is lust without love or
law. It is evil. A person who is tempering, shaping and controlling this great
creative force to serve God and humanity is governed by the *yetser ha tov*. This
second person builds a house, takes a spouse and begets children, helps others,
worships the One and Only God.

In a frank self-revealing statement the great and productive Jewish writer
Isaac Bashevis Singer said: "I lived yet was ashamed to live, ashamed to eat
and ashamed to go to the outhouse. I longed for sex and I was ashamed of
my passions." (cited in Schwarz, p. 107) We know that Singer controlled
and sublimated his creative force into literature for which he won the Nobel
Prize. He gave the answer to my question about how to eliminate the evil
inclination: we don't eliminate it. Our life is a never-ending effort to control
and channel it. Rabbi Jose the Galilean said that the struggle against the evil
inclination creates greatness in humans. "The Evil Inclination incites scholars
'more than anyone else'..." and "The greater the man the greater is his [Evil]
Inclination." (Cited in Urbach, *The Sages*, p. 476) This means that a person
struggles to direct the creative force toward good; if successful, he or she may
produce a great idea, beautiful art and music, a cure for disease. Or he or she
may become a loving parent, son or daughter, teacher, partner and friend.

This all means that the first step in channeling the creative force toward good is the unambiguous affirmation of our own love for God and for other human beings. The second is asking God for help. That is the answer to my question about how to struggle with the guilt we feel because of *yetser ha ra*. Love is the weapon.

In the third paragraph of the daily *Sh'ma* prayer there is the warning about lust, but the emphasis at the beginning of this prayer is love: "And you shall love the Lord your God with all your heart, with all your soul, and with all your might." (Deut 6:4-5) In short, before we read about the dangers of lust (Num 15:39) we read about love. Since we know that God created human beings in His own image, the love we express toward God through study, prayer and obedience must be accompanied by love for humans; the love we express toward another human being through good deeds, kindness, respect and intimacy must be accompanied by love for God.

I would have liked to say that this is enough, but we mortals are not strong enough. We need God's help, and that is why we pray to Him in the preliminary morning service: "let not the evil impulse have power over us… make us cling to the good impulse and to good deeds, and bend our will to submit to Thee." Armed with our own love and with God's help, we can control and direct the force, the *yetser*, toward loving, constructive acts.

# 38

## *Korach*

✦

## *(Numbers 16:1-18:32)\**

Within a relatively short period of time four insurrections threaten Moses. Two of them are counterrevolutionary in the sense that their leaders reject Moses, and they deny God's plan to settle the Israelites in the Promised Land. The first comes after the negative report by the spies in Parashat *Sh'lach L'kha* when people say: "Let us appoint a chief [meaning someone different from Moses] and let us return to Egypt." (Num 14:4) According to Jewish legend, Dathan and Abiram of the tribe of Reuben are the preferred new leaders (Ginzberg, p. 276). Seizing this opportunity, Dathan and Abiram lead the second insurrection which we read about in Parashat *Korach*. They claim that life was better in Egypt and want to return thereby denying "the whole Divine origin of [Moses'] mission as well as the special relation of God to Israel."(Hirsch on Num 5:15, pp. 279-280). These are most definitely counterrevolutionary movements.

The third insurrection is an attempted coup d'état. Korach, a Levite, who is Moses' cousin, accepts the Covenant. He believes in God's promises, but he is angry with Moses and says that power and prestige should be more widely shared. Specifically, he opposes the appointment of Moses' brother Aaron and Aaron's descendants as priests. It would be easy to dismiss Korach as merely jealous of his cousins' prestige and power, but there is more to Korach's motives than simple jealousy as I shall point out.

The fourth revolt is a result of the punishment of Dathan and Abiram who are swallowed into the earth and the punishment of the followers of Korach who are burned to death. The masses of people are shocked by the sudden and brutal death of their leaders which they witness. They begin to rail against Moses and Aaron: "The two of you have caused the death of the people of God." (Num 17:6) They menace Moses and Aaron and might have killed them had it not been for a plague unleashed by the Almighty. To Moses'

111

credit he orders Aaron to make expiation for the Israelites, and Aaron protects almost all of them by the smoke from incense.

As I mentioned earlier, Korach's challenge to Moses is different from the other three challenges in that he opposes individuals, not the Covenant. In my view, his challenge has some merit. To defend Korach I shall answer the following four questions: Who was Korach? Why does he oppose Moses and Aaron? Did Korach achieve anything from his attempted coup d'état? What implications do Korach's initiatives have for us?

## 1. Who was Korach?

Korach, a respected and influential leader of the Levites, was the son of Yitzhar the younger brother of Amram, Moses' and Aaron's father. According to Midrash, in Egypt before the exodus he was already an important person because he worked in the king's palace and amassed a sizeable fortune. (*Midrash Rabbah Numbers,* XVIII:15) At Sinai he was most probably in the forefront of the Levites who rallied to Moses and who killed the worshippers of the golden calf made by Aaron. In this week's Parashah his ability to recruit 250 Israelite leaders presumably from all the tribes to challenge Moses proves his considerable influence. Midrash calls these 250 men "all the chiefs of Israel and the Sanhedrin…" (*Midrash Rabbah Numbers,* XVIII:3)

Korach is married and has three sons who with many other descendants will play important roles in Israelite history long after the supposed demise of Korach. I say "supposed demise" because when the 250 followers of Korach offer burning incense to the Lord, as Moses instructed them to do, "a fire went forth from the Lord and consumed [them]" (Num 16:15). The text does not explicitly include Korach. (For differing views, see Sanhedrin 110a)

## 2. Why does Korach oppose Moses and Aaron?

He is already in a bad mood because another Levite, Elzaphon, a man junior to him in the tribe, has been appointed to a leadership position to which Korach aspired (*Midrash Rabbah, Numbers,* XVIII:2, p. 708). But, what instigates his rebellion that we read about in this Parashah is the appointment of Moses' brother as priest. Korach explains his opposition in the most simple and direct way: he says to Moses "*Rav lachem*" (Num16:3) The *Etz Hayim* Chumash translates this phrase as "You have gone too far," A clearer translation would be"You take too much" or "you have too much" (Alter, p. 763, ftn. 7; Fox, p. 737) Korach has accepted one son of Amram, namely Moses, as leader, but he balks at the appointment of another member of the Amram family, namely Aaron, as high priest. It is not only Aaron, the individual that he opposes. He realizes that the family of Aaron, to be called the House of Aaron, will be ensconced in power as priests for all time.

Korach must have been sincere when he claimed that all Israel - not just the sons of Amram – is holy. He implied – possibly as a tactic to recruit allies for himself from other tribes - that the priesthood should rotate among the tribes.

Korach is also offended by the subordinate political and economic role the Levites will play after the creation of the Aaronide priesthood. Levite men from the age of 25 to the age of 50 will serve the Aaronides in the Sanctuary as guards, porters of the Sanctuary in the desert, musicians, doorkeepers; they will also become teachers and judges but only as assistants to the Aaronides. Unlike the other tribes, they will have no land in the Promised Land, which means their wealth and their incomes will be restricted to a portion of the offerings that the Israelites bring to the Sanctuary. In a somewhat condescending way, Moses will ask the Israelites to tithe their farm produce for the benefit of the Levites, the stranger, the fatherless and the widow once every three years. (Deut 14:27-29) Levites will be granted cities after settlement in the Promised Land, but we read in the Book of Joshua that the Aaronides get a proportionately large share of them. (Joshua 21: thirteen out of twenty three cities, from. *Jewish Encyclopedia.Com,* "Kohath")

Thirdly, Korach is offended by the requirement that Levite men who are not priests must completely shave their heads, their beards and bodies thereby removing outward signs of their masculinity. According to Jewish legend, Korach's wife mocks his appearance (Ginzberg,Vol. III, p. 288).

## 3. Did Korach achieve anything for the Levites?

According to Robert Michels' famous "iron law of oligarchy, "a small group of people will eventually emerge to govern any organization or institution. If rule by the few is inevitable, their legitimacy or acceptance depends on their behavior toward the general population: how open or closed are they to recruits from outside their own families. Are they authoritarian or do they respond to the wishes of the people? Do they accept diversity or do they attempt to impose conformity? How do they deal with challenges to their policies and power? Are they corrupt?

Korach perceives the beginnings of an authoritarian oligarchy, which he opposes, and he perceives that Moses is not so modest as he is usually portrayed. At the core of the nascent oligarchy are Moses, Aaron, Aaron's two sons Eleazar and Ithamar, Aaron's grandson Pinchas, plus Joshua and Caleb. Caleb, according to Jewish legend, was the perfect sycophant giving Moses all the credit for leading the Israelites from Egypt, for parting the sea, for giving Israel manna in the desert (Ginzberg,Vol III, p.273).

This entourage should probably include the ten spies – in addition to Joshua and Caleb – about whom we read in Parashat *Sh'lach L'kha*. None of them was a tribal prince who had been "consecrated with the holy anointing oil…" (Cited by Jeffrey Cohen, p. 221). Rather, they were lower ranking tribal leaders different from the men chosen by God at the beginning of the Book of Numbers to conduct the census and whom God calls "the princes" (Numbers 1:16). It is not unreasonable to speculate that Moses was counting on these subordinate men to support him in the years to come. He was, of course, surprised at their negative report. And, even worse for Moses, his choices provoked the anger of the higher ranking princes who consequently supported Korach. (Jeffrey Cohen, p. 227)

Moses reacts decisively to the challenge to his authority. Keeping information about God's choice of Aaron to himself, which is typical authoritarian behavior, he says that the Levites already have enough honor because they will serve in the Sanctuary. Moses refuses to recognize any of Korach's interests and devises a clever plan to rid himself of Korach and his supporters. He knows full well what happened to Aaron's sons who offered unauthorized fire at the altar. Without consulting the Almighty he tells Korach's supporters to offer burning incense before the altar. The fact that Korach and his supporters quickly accepted Moses' challenge proves they were unaware of God's choice of Aaron as high priest. Because of their devotion to God and the Covenant, they "were sure that this trial by ordeal would prove their case and vindicate their cause." (Green, p. 79) They did not perceive themselves as rebels.

The most important sign of Moses' growing sense of his own preeminence is revealed in Parashat *Chukkat* when the people demand water. Although God told him to speak to the rock, Moses struck it with his staff after telling the people "shall we [meaning Aaron and himself] get water for you out of this rock?" (Num 20:10) Thus, Moses takes credit for the water which gushes forth. In the words of Jacob Milgrom, Moses ascribes "the miracle to his own powers." (Milgrom, p.422). For this "usurpation" (the word is Milgrom's) of God's powers Moses will be punished by not being allowed to enter the Promised Land.

Despite the crushing of Korach's attempted coup, some concessions will be made to the Levites. One concession is symbolic. In this Parashah, Israel is reminded that the Aaronides and Moses are and remain Levites. The tribal leaders are instructed to give their wooden staves to Moses who will place them in the Sanctuary. The staff that sprouts leaves and blossoms will be the staff of the man chosen by God as priest. Aaron's name is inscribed on the

Levites' staff which duly sprouts leaves and blossoms showing, according to Hirsch, that "Jewish priests do not cease to be Levites...." They are the elite of the tribe. (Hirsch on Numbers 17:18, p. 292) Moreover, neither the Levites as a whole nor the Aaronides as priests are superior to other Israelites. Hirsch says they are to be seen as the vanguard whose role is to lead the "spiritual and general development of life." (Hirsch on Numbers 17:24, p. 294)

Another concession to Korach is that his three sons, who are said to have dissociated themselves from the rebellion and to have repented for it, are permitted to survive. They play important roles in Israel's future. They compose several psalms. Korach's most famous descendant is Samuel. Samuel, the Levite, (Rashi on I Samuel 1:1, in Rosenberg, p. 3) ruled Israel in the interim between the disgrace and downfall of the priesthood at Shilo and the creation of the monarchy and a rejuvenated priesthood. Evidence from the  First Book of Chronicles (I Chron 9:19) as well as inscriptions found by archaeologists prove that in time there would be an important House of Korach as Korach wished. (Levine, 429 – 430)

## 4. What are the implications of Korach's revolt?

First, the rebellion of Korach is a sign of the uncertainties within any society undergoing reorganization. The children of Israel grew into a people in Egypt in terms of numbers; as they progress toward the Promised Land God is giving them an infrastructure and identity with the commandments, institutions, rules and a hierarchy of authority based on differing relationships with the Sanctuary which contains the alters and tablets of the Covenant. Observing the four rebellions and the brutal punishments, the people are desperately confused about their own relationship with the Sanctuary. They lament (Num 17:27): "We are lost, all of us lost...we are doomed to perish." The Almighty is trying to explain that the high priest can approach the Ark of the Covenant; the other priests approach the alters with sacrifices; the Levites guard the outer perimeters; and all the other Israelites bring sacrifices to the Levites and priests. Altogether, they are the Chosen People. In the Books of Leviticus and Numbers the rules and regulations are being set forth as they must be in any newly formed society or newly independent state. Another painful reorganization will take place later with the creation of the monarchy.

The second implication is the danger of a closed authoritarian oligarchy. It is true that petty motives and jealousy may motivate opposition to leaders, who are necessary in any institution, but more important issues are also at stake. Diverse opinions and practices may enrich communities and institutions; they may bring about needed changes within the context of the Covenant.

An authoritarian and exclusive group of leaders running secular and religious institutions risks driving people away from these institutions. They may even alienate Jews from the Jewish people and state. For these reasons the oligarchs are a greater threat to the children of Israel than is Korach.

*An earlier version of this chapter appeared as "In Defense of Korach" in the *Jewish Bible Quarterly*, Vol.37, No. 4, 2009, pp. 259-264. Published with permission of JBQ.

# 39

## *Chukkat*

✦

### *(Numbers 19:1-22:1)*

A momentous change in the life of Moses takes place in this Parashah. The people are complaining about the lack of water; they exasperate Moses with their complaints. In spite of everything they have seen and experienced, they dare to ask him: "Why did you make us leave Egypt to bring us to this wretched place…?" (Num 20:5)

Moses, along with his brother Aaron, appeals to God for help. God instructs Moses and Aaron to take the staff, which they have used before to perform miracles, to stand in front of a rock and in the presence of all the Israelites to command "the rock to yield its water." (Num 20:8). Instead of following the Lord's instructions to the letter, Moses, who must have been very angry, shouts to all the people "Listen, you rebels, shall we get water for you out of this rock?" (Num 20:10) He then strikes the rock with the staff – rather than commanding the rock - and copious water flows from the rock.

He has violated the Lord's instructions. He struck the rock instead of speaking to it, and he implied that he and Aaron were responsible for obtaining the water. His anger was also a sin according to Maimonides because the Israelites might "imagine the Deity was a cruel forbidding God and not the Compassionate Father of all, hastening to quench the thirst of His people by commanding water from the flinty rock." (Leibowitz, p. 240)

The Lord responds to these actions by accusing Moses and Aaron of not trusting the Lord and not affirming the Lord's sanctity and responsibility for the water to the Israelites. God then tells Moses and Aaron that they will be punished. Neither will enter the Promised Land.

In the course of this Parashah both Aaron and his sister Miriam die and we can conclude that Moses' life will be spared only until the Israelites are ready to cross the Jordan. Thus, the three siblings – Moses, Aaron and Miriam – are destined by God to disappear from the community of Israel. Aaron's descendants will continue their duties in the Tabernacle, but descendants of Moses and Miriam seem to vanish. Why can't the Almighty forgive Moses? Why doesn't He allow these three leaders to enter the Land of Israel? I think the answer can be found by going back to look at the incident of the Golden Calf.

Remember that when Moses ascends Mount Sinai to receive the commandments, the Israelites are so afraid of being abandoned that they demand that Aaron create an image for them: "Come, make us a god who shall go before us, for that man Moses, who brought us from the land of Egypt – we do not know what has happened to him." (Ex 32:1) According to Rashbam (Rabbi Sh'muel ben Meir, circa 1085-circa 1174), the Israelites believed that God had actually produced the golden calf as "a replacement for Moses, and if they would now carry the golden calf in front of them, or have it walk in front of them, this would be equivalent to having the holy spirit walking ahead of them." (Rashbam on Ex 32:4, cited in *Hachut Hamushulash*, Vol 4, p. 1159) There is no reason for them to assume that God had abandoned them, but they feel they need an intermediary in the absence of Moses. Three thousand people are killed for this mistake.

These two incidents, the golden calf and the striking of the rock, show that God understands that human beings may slip into worship of one leader, and leaders may begin to think of themselves as infallible and all-powerful. God is sending us a warning. By punishing the Israelites, God tries to prevent them from deifying one person, and by refusing Moses entry into the Promised Land, God demonstrates to leaders the limits of their power. Eventually we learn to live without any intermediary between ourselves and God. Eventually secular and religious leaders who believe in their own infallibility learn the risks of this delusion to themselves and their followers.

# 40

## *Balak*

✦

### *(Numbers 22:2-25:9)*

Balak, King of the Moabites, hired Balaam to curse and thus to stop the Israelite advance into Moabite territory on their way to the Promised Land. In one of the most memorable stories in the Book of Numbers Balaam fails at first, but he seems to have contrived a scheme for Moabite women to seduce Israelite men that we read about at the end of the Parashah.

Interesting aspects of this story are two extra-biblical discoveries by archaeologists. According to scholars, Balaam, son of Beor, lived in western Asia as a leader with reputed supernatural powers. Some evidence for his life and influence comes from an inscription on a wall plaster found at Tell Deir 'Alla in the Kingdom of Jordan. The inscription dates from between the 7th and 9th centuries BCE but may refer to an earlier period. It begins as follows: "(The) Book of Balaam, son of Beor, a man who saw the gods." (de Tarragon, p. 2073) He dreams about impending disaster to his people quite possibly from the Israelites. (Greene, p. x and passim) This inscription does not conform exactly to the text from Tanakh, but it is close enough to imply reactions of the peoples of Canaan and its environs to the advent of the Israelites.

Other extra-biblical evidence shows the interaction between Israel and its neighbors. For example, a stele or inscribed stone dating from 830 BCE celebrates a Moabite victory over Israel: "As for Omri, King of Israel, he humbled Moab many years... but I [King Mesha of Moab] triumphed over Israel. Israel has perished forever." (Blenkinsopp, p. 1309)

In this Parashah Balaam is mocked. The Almighty gives him permission to go to accept his assignment from King Balak and then blocks him from acting. More important, his donkey is able to see an angel sent by God, but at first he cannot see it. (Num 22:22-27)

He meets King Balak, his employer, but he is made to look powerless because of his failure to weaken the Israelites. The sites chosen for the cursing were apparently Canaanite and Moabite cultic centers or shrines. The last one of them, Peor, was a place of sanctity and awe for the peoples of Canaan, but the deity can do nothing against Israel. (Num 23:28-30) Balaam is forced to bless Israel. King Balak dismisses him.

Before Balaam departs he explains to the Moabites that God's protection will not allow cursing of Israel, but he suggests that Israelite men are weak and can be seduced by Moabite women. (Num 31:16) This allegation is repeated in the Christian Bible wherein it is said that Balaam succeeded in secretly showing how the Israelites could be led to self-destruct by angering God. ("Revelation to John," 2:14)

It seems to work to the advantage of the Moabites, for many Israelite men permit themselves to be seduced at Peor by Moabite women who during their intimate encounters sacrificed to and worshipped Moabite idols. (Num 25:1-4) As Milgrom puts it, the Israelites began to engage "in sacrificial feasts of the god Baal-peor." (Milgrom, p. 480) God promptly punishes them with a plague which ceases only when Aaron's grandson, Pinchas, kills an Israelite man and a Moabite woman in *flagrant delit*. Pinchas saves Israel from God's anger.

The archaeological evidence for the Moabites and Balaam is not important even though it is often satisfying to find it in scientific books and articles. What is important is that Israelite doubts and disobedience are their worst enemies. Milgrom writes that "because this was the first such Israelite encounter with the culture of Canaan and because the devastating plague was attributed to divine wrath, Baal-peor came to be etched in the collective memory as a nadir in Israel's history." (Milgrom, p. 480).

Psalm 106 (7-39) lists Baal-Peor and seven other episodes of Israelite apostasy after their departure from Egypt. They are:

1. Doubting God when they reached the Sea of Reeds.
2. Doubting God in the wilderness.
3. Revolting against Moses.
4. Making the golden calf
5. Rejecting the Promised Land after the spies' report.
6. Rebelling against Moses at the waters of Meribah.
7. Intermingling with other nations, worshipping their idols, and copying their ways.

What prevent the destruction of Israel after each episode are partly leadership, partly repentance, and partly the Lord's love for Israel. Even the Lord's condemnation of the Moabites for their treachery (Deut 23:4-6) is mitigated somewhat by the fact the Ruth, a Moabite, becomes part of the tribe of Judah. By giving birth to a son, Obed, she is an ancestor of King David. (Cf. Book of Ruth)

Despite Israelite disobedience; despite implacable enemies, Israel survives. Each generation is faced with a challenge. We understand that an understanding of the particular challenge in one's time and place is the first step in meeting and conquering it.

# 41

## *Pinchas*

◆

### *(Numbers 25:10-30:1)*

At the very end of last week's Parashah, Pinchas, a grandson of Aaron, killed a prominent Israelite and his idolatrous lover, a Moabite, thus stopping the plague which was devastating the Israelites. In this Parashah, God expresses His approval for Pinchas' action and tells Moses "I grant him - Pinchas - My pact of friendship. It shall be for him and his descendants after him a pact of priesthood for all time, because he took impassioned action for his God, thus making expiation for the Israelites. "(Num 25:12-13) The Parashah is appropriately named after Pinchas. Pinchas' branch of Aaron's descendants thereby becomes "the exclusive officiants in the Temple." (Milgrom, pp. 216-217, ftn. 13.)

The lesson to us is clear. There are many enemies like King Balak and his hired sorcerer, Balaam, about whom we have already read, who will try to thwart the Israelites from achieving their goals. Even off the battlefield they will try to find ways to undermine the Covenant between Israel and the Almighty. For these reasons, the Israelites must be prepared for more battles of all kinds, and they must always have talented leaders who understand the relationship between Israel and God.

Consequently, the Lord instructs Moses to take a census to determine the number of fighting men. Then the Almighty explains how the Promised Land is going to be divided up according to male leaders of tribes and tribal factions. Some women come forward to protest that they should not be excluded because there is no male head of their family. God resolves the problem: "If a man dies without leaving a son, you shall transfer his property to his daughter." (Num 27:8)

At this point the Israelites are on the east side of the River Jordan not far from Jericho, within sight of the Promised Land. The Lord tells Moses to climb a mountain in order to view the land which he will never enter. Moses is disappointed that he will never live in Israel, but, true to his devotion to his people, he requests that God appoint someone else to take his place, someone "who shall take them out and bring them in, so that the Lord's community may not be like sheep that have no shepherd." (Num 27:17) God tells him that Joshua is that person, and Moses introduces him to the priests and the Israelites as his successor. Joshua has already proven that he is loyal and courageous. In sight of everyone Moses put his hands on Joshua proclaiming him to be the future leader of Israel. (Num 27:23)

We see that leadership is an important theme of this Parashah. Moses is the ever-present leader, but he seems unable to act when the Israelite men are seduced by the idol worshipping Moabites. Pinchas takes the initiative and saves the Israelites from annihilation. God then legitimizes Pinchas as a spiritual leader while Joshua will become their secular leader resolving the day to day problems of the people.

Different types of leader of the community are emerging: the one who is chosen directly by God - Moses; the one who is self-selected, who rises up when the situation demands resolute, fearless behavior - Pinchas; the leaders who inherit their position - the priests; and the leaders who prove themselves by their courage and loyalty - Joshua. Beginning with Moses, it is clear that no leaders are perfect, for they are human beings just like the rest of us; no leader can do everything perfectly. Although Jews are taught to respect community leaders, we are also taught not to worship them.

# 42

## *Mattot*

♦

### *(Numbers 30:2-32:42)*

Vengeance is an important topic in the Tanakh. God commands the Israelites to take vengeance – *nakam* - on the Midianites. These people, who are identified with the Moabites, must be punished for having tried to destroy God's covenant with Israel. After their hired diviner Balaam failed to curse Israel they sent women to seduce Israelite men into cult shrines for rituals of sex and idol worship which, of course, violated the commandments. Pinchas saved Israel from disaster, and afterwards Moses conveys God's message to kill the Midianites: "Let men be picked out from among you for a campaign, and let them fall upon Midian to wreak the Lord's vengeance on Midian." (Num 31:3) In this Parashah Israel is the instrument of God's vengeance.

Individuals sometimes ask God to be the instrument of their own vengeance. The prophet Jeremiah complained to God that there were people who constantly attacked him. He asked the Lord to wreak His vengeance upon them: "my persecutors shall stumble...O Lord of Hosts...Let me see Your retribution upon them." (Jer 20:11-12)

God is usually the direct avenger for God's own purposes. For example, God promises to take vengeance on the nations which have persecuted Israel because, as Rashi put it, whoever "attacks Israel is as though he attacks the Holy One, blessed be He." (Rashi on Num 31:3)

Individuals and institutions also take revenge without reference to or authorization from the Almighty. The question is when is such action justified?

All forms of vengeance may be defined as "the impulse to retaliate when wrongs are done." (Minow, p. 10) The reasoning is that wrongdoing must be punished in some way in order to reaffirm moral principles and to "express our basic self-respect." (Minow, p. 10) The psalmist puts the same idea in a different albeit harsh way: "The righteous man will rejoice when he sees revenge." (Ps 58:11)

The Psalms tell us further that the righteous person will "execute vengeance upon the nations...." (Ps 149:7) I shall give two examples from the Bible and one example from contemporary history. First, Simeon and Levi kill Shechem for having abused their sister, Dinah. They take revenge in the name of family honor, as they explain to their nonplussed father (Gen 34: 26 -31) Second, in the Book of Judges we read that Sisera a Canaanite army commander who "had oppressed Israel ruthlessly for twenty years." (Judges 4:3) sought refuge in the tent of Yael, wife of Heber the Kenite. She offered him drink, and, according to some interpretations, (See Kalmanofsky, p. 22, ftn. 15) she also offered her body. While he slept she killed him. Israelites then celebrated by singing "Most blessed of women be Yael...She struck Sisera, crushed his head....At her feet he sank...." (Judges 5:24-27) I shall return to the story of Yael later.

From our own times there is the example of Ms. Ankie Spitzer who made a different choice. In September 1972 eleven Israeli athletes were taken hostage by Black September, a Palestinian terrorist organization, at the Olympic Games in Munich. During an inept rescue operation by the German police the terrorists killed all of the athletes. Spitzer, widow of one Israeli athlete, eschewed violence. "I don't live for revenge, I live for justice," she said. (Reeve, p. 186) By justice she meant that she wanted the terrorists to be brought to trial, and she wanted full disclosure by the Germans about what they had done and what they had failed to do.

On 21st June 1964 civil rights workers Andrew Goodman, Michael Schwerner and James Earl Chaney were murdered in Mississippi. Exactly 41 years later one of their murderers was convicted in a Mississippi court. The mother of Andrew Goodman said about the murderer: "I just hope he's off the streets. I don't want anything more terrible than that. I don't want anything violent. I'm against capital punishment." (CNN.com)

Governments cannot easily avoid robust action against terrorists because they have to protect their populations. The Israeli government felt it had to react to the murder of Israeli athletes with violence. Shortly after the Munich disaster the government of Prime Minister Golda Meir launched "Operation Wrath of God" to assassinate terrorists involved directly and indirectly in the Olympic massacres. One member of the Israeli assassination squad said: "This operation...was aimed to punish those who planned and committed this crime.... I think that every nation that respects itself should know how to punish those who harm them." (Reeve, p. 183)

What are the dangers and risks of revenge? One act of revenge might start a cycle of violence. After Simeon and Levi take revenge on Shechem, their father Jacob, fearing attack from his neighbors, moves the family away. The operation initiated by Israel as revenge for the murders of Israeli athletes succeeded in killing several Palestinian terrorists. Palestinians responded by killing Israelis. During rounds of vengeance the Israelis mistakenly killed a Moroccan waiter in Norway. The Palestinians mistakenly killed air passengers in Athens.

Another risk is that the avenger might violate commandments. (Green, e-mail) For example, Yael, the Kenite who killed Sisera, may have committed adultery, and she certainly murdered a man who posed no threat to her as a non-Israelite. In the 2004 Israeli film *Walk on Water* when an experienced Israeli agent hesitates to murder an infamous Nazi criminal, the Nazi's grandson decides to takes revenge on behalf of the Jewish people by killing his own grandfather.

What are the implications? Because of the risks of violence and sin, we could take the view that violent vengeance must be left to God or some judicial institution. Individuals such as Ms. Spitzer, and the families of Schwerner, Goodman and Chaney had some choice in how they reacted to wrongdoing. They eschewed personal vengeance and looked to the courts. Jews as a people are not always given such a choice. The Israeli government felt it had no choice other than tracking the terrorists down and killing them on the spot.

The answer to my first question about when vengeance is justified is that holy texts and rabbinic commentary restrict individual and institutional vengeance to well-defined examples. In chapter 21 of Exodus: "He who fatally strikes a man shall be put to death." (Ex 21:12) According to Rabbi Dr. Yosef Green's analysis, however, "revenge is prohibited in the Holiness Code (Lev 19:18 – 'You shall not take vengeance...') The Septuagint translation of Leviticus 19:18 is 'you shall not take the law into your own hands.' The Qumram community took Leviticus 19:18 to mean that God alone is to take vengeance on His enemies. We find in the *Midrash Hagadol* the following: 'Indeed it is distinctly taught that man should not imitate God in the following four things, which He alone can use as instruments. They are jealousy, revenge, exaltation and acting in devious ways.'" (Green, e-mail) As difficult as it may be, Maimonides wrote that in secular matters a person should "practice forebearance." (Green citing *Mishneh Torah De'ot*, vii,7)

My second question is about risks. Yael murdered and may have committed adultery; the young German murdered; the Israelis and Palestinians murdered, but there is no evidence that God told them to commit adultery and murder. Didn't all of them sin by violating commandments? Or, could they be excused by claiming they sinned "for the sake of God" just as the Israelites sinned by killing the Midianites?

In an article in the journal *Conservative Judaism,* Rabbi Jeffrey Kalmanofsky examined actions which, in his opinion, amounted to sinning for God by violating commandments. His arguments depend on the statements of the Talmudic sage Rabbi Nachman b. Yitzchak. With reference to Yael, Rav Nachman said: (Nazir 23b) "Greater is a sin for God's sake than a *mitzvah* for ulterior motives." On the basis of Rabbi Nachman's laconic statement, Kalmanofsky posits dialectic between God's law and God's will; he says Yael "discerned God's will...even as it clashed with the law." (Kalmanofsky, p. 11) Saving Israelite lives and saving the Covenant with God were more important than strict obedience to the law. (Kalmanofsky, p.15)

Along the same lines of thought Rabbi Abraham Joshua Heschel wrote "*Halakhah* must not be observed for its own sake, but for the sake of God. The law must not be idolized. It is a part, not all, of the Torah. We live and die for the sake of God rather than for the sake of the law." (cited by Kalmanofsky, p. 24) Asserting that an understanding of the will of God trumps an understanding of *Halakhah* is rich in risks and possibilities. The problem with that point of view is that many can claim they understand the will of God and then proceed to commit acts that are against the laws of the Torah and secular society. Isn't chaos a possible outcome?

Vengeance is an important and problematic topic in the Bible. It is not obvious when individual or group initiatives of vengeance would be approved by God. The message in this Parashah is, in any case, not really about punishing enemies; it is rather about survival – survival in order to serve the Almighty. It is God's will that Jews survive as a dynamic community governed by God's laws as interpreted through the generations. One might conclude that Jews and the Jewish state have the right to fight those who threaten Jewish survival.

Vengeance as self-defense is a possible instrument; it is not in any way central to Jewish existence.

Jews do not define themselves as victims focusing attention on revenge for past crimes or potential future crimes against the Jewish people or state. We define ourselves and we thrive as a people by vigorously affirming our Covenant with the Almighty; by joyously claiming our traditions; by creatively adapting *Halakhah* to our times; and most of all by humbly endeavoring to understand and to follow God's will.

# 43

## *Mas'ei*

♦

## *(Numbers 33:1-36:13)*

Moses fills many roles for us. In this last Parashah of the Book of Numbers, Moses is our national historian. He relates the last forty years of wandering by reminding us that the Israelites started from Egypt; after many stages or *Mas'ei*, the name of the Parashah, they have finally arrived to the eastern bank of the Jordan River, just across from the Promised Land. The text says: "Moses recorded the starting points of their various marches as directed by the Lord."(Num 33:2) Why all these details?

Ramban explains the reasons for this written record by quoting Maimonides who wrote that later generations might not believe this story. The land between Egypt and Israel is so inhospitable that people could not survive without some miracles. The miracles of the manna and the water must be recorded "so that the future generations would see them and acknowledge the great wonders [entailed] in keeping people alive in such places for forty years." (Ramban on Num 33:1)

After telling the story of the marches toward the Promised Land, Moses delineates the frontiers of the Land. Its western border is "the coast of the Great Sea" (Num 34:6) and its eastern border extends along the Jordan River. The Jordan River is a symbol of the history that Moses tells us about.

The name "Jordan" probably means descending or downward. The river originates from the confluence of streams in the mountains between Israel, Syria and Lebanon. It meanders 200 miles to the small Lake Huleh where today there is a fantastic nature reserve, then to the Kinneret or Sea of Galilee and then to the Dead Sea. It is the most important source of potable water for Israel, the Palestinian territories, as well as for the Kingdom of Jordan.

We read about the river first in the Book of Genesis when Abraham and his nephew Lot go their separate ways. Lot chooses to live near the Jordan because of the well watered land.

In the Book of Joshua the first message from God to Joshua is "Moses, my servant is dead, now therefore arise, cross over the Jordan, you and this entire people, to the land which I gave to them, to the people of Israel." (Josh 1:2) After the children of Israel cross the Jordan River, their lives change radically because they have finally entered into their own land. The association of the Jordan River with change is mentioned in the Talmud: a leper is cured after bathing in the river. These waters also have a special significance for Christians as John baptized people there. (Mat 3:6)

The River Jordan separates the past from the future. The east side, where the Israelites in this Parashah are encamped, represents the forty years of wandering, the past; the west side is the Promised Land, the future where the Promised Land becomes the Land of Israel.

An Israeli political leader once said that if Israelis and Jews only look in the rear view mirror while driving cars, they are going to crash into what is coming down the road. By analogy, as a people we have to think about the past, but Jews must keep their eyes resolutely on the future. That is what the Torah teaches us. It is both a history which helps us understand our identity and our role in the world as well as a guide for our lives as individuals and as a people. Put another way, Jews look in the rear view mirror from time to time to understand the stages or marches – the *Mas'ei* – of existence, but Jews study Torah because Jews are a modern and forward looking people committed to life.

# D'VARIM/DEUTERONOMY

# 44

## D'varim

✦

### (Deuteronomy 1:1-3:22)

This Parashah marks the beginning of the fifth and last book of Torah, *D'varim* or Deuteronomy. "These are the words [*d'varim*] that Moses addressed to all Israel on the other side of the Jordan." (Deut. 1:1) Moses knows his mission is coming to an end, and he wants to repeat the main points of Torah to his followers. In fact, this book is often called *Mishneh Torah* or "Repetition of the Torah" because Moses summarizes the commandments and Israel's history.

Some sages have written that while the first four books of Torah are the words of God faithfully recorded by Moses, the last book is the voice of Moses reflecting on his experiences and his personal feelings about the Israelite nation. Moses orders future leaders to read Deuteronomy aloud during a gathering of the whole nation once every seven years. (Deut 31:10-11) He wants Jews to study Deuteronomy because the book is far more than a summary. In fact, Moses is trying to transmit a method to ensure Jewish survival, a very important issue this time of the Jewish year, about seven weeks before Rosh Hashana.

This Parashah is read the week before *Tish'a b'Av* - the 9th of Av, the day on which the two Temples in Jerusalem were destroyed, a terrible calamity threatening Jewish existence as a people in a covenantal relationship with the Almighty. The Haftarah portion comes from Isaiah beginning with the following words: "The vision of Isaiah, the son of Amoz which he saw concerning Judah and Jerusalem....." (Isaiah 1:1) The word "vision" is *chazon* in Hebrew, and, therefore, this is the name given to this Sabbath.

What did Isaiah see? What was his vision? The answer is that the prophet saw destruction and suffering. Isaiah says that because Israel refused to obey God, "Your land is a waste, Your cities burnt down; Before your eyes, the yield of your soil is consumed by strangers - A wasteland as if overthrown by strangers!" (Isaiah 1:7) We get a similar vision from *The Book of Lamentations* which is read very solemnly on *Tish'a b'Av.* "[God] has let the foe rejoice over you, Has exalted the might of your enemies." (Lamentations 2:17)

Moses himself has predicted this disaster in the Book of Deuteronomy because he knew there would be times when the Israelites would fail to keep their obligations toward God. The morning of *Tish'a b'Av* the Torah reading includes Moses' warning that if Israel worships idols, as Moses expects Israel to do, "you shall soon perish from the land that you are crossing the Jordan to possess; you shall not long endure in it, but shall be utterly wiped out. The Lord will scatter you among the peoples, and only a scant few of you shall be left among the nations to which the Lord will drive you." (Deut 4:26-27) Obedience to the commandments will ensure redemption, but how to reach that goal is the question.

The way to obedience begins with study of the texts transmitted by Moses and then the application of these texts to one's daily life. In Deuteronomy Moses gives Israel a method for obedience through study, writing and application. Although Moses refers to his text as a summary, much from the previous four books is left out such as the creation of the world, Adam and Eve, No-ach, Joseph, the near sacrifice of Isaac and the centrality of the priests and Temple.

According to Jeffrey H. Tigay, Moses includes 200 essential laws some of which are not included in the previous four books: the *Sh'ma, Amidah, Aleinu,* the *Haggadah,* public reading of Torah, blessings after meals, *kiddush, kashrut, mezuzot, tsitsit,* wearing *tefillin,* and mourning procedures. (Tigay, p. xxviii) Moses' focus is on the people and their personal observance and behavior without intermediaries such as priests. In this last book of the Torah the word "holy" is almost exclusively used with reference to the Israelite people rather than for places or institutions.

Moses knew Jews would face disasters such as the loss of the Temple on the 9th of Av. He provided them a means for preservation and renewal, namely, Torah study and commentary. Although Jews believe that all five books of the Torah come from God, the last book, Deuteronomy, is also the first commentary on Torah. God through Moses legitimizes this intellectual process. When Jews search for answers to contemporary questions, they study Torah with the help of Talmud, Midrash, Rabbinic *Responsa* (answers to questions), modern Bible scholarship and the human intellect. Commentary, as defined very broadly, is the result.

Saadia Gaon, (882-942) head of the Sura Academy at Baghdad during the 10th century, wrote that Jews must analyze theological questions in a rational way. He explained that "God has graciously transmitted the essential truths through his prophets. Despite this, the confirmation provided by reason is valuable, both for the believers themselves, to have confirmed in our intellect what we have learned from the prophet of God theoretically, and in order to enable them to refute the arguments of those who attack their religion." (Brody, p. 292)

Torah commentary, first legitimized by Moses in the Book of Deuteronomy, helps Jews to understand and resolve problems in their relationship with God, with other peoples, with the Jewish past and with the Jewish future in the State of Israel and in the Diaspora. It ensures the vitality of Judaism and Torah from generation to generation.

# 45

## *Va-etchannan*

✦

### *(Deuteronomy. 3:23-7:11)*

This Parashah is read during the first Shabbat after 9ᵗʰ of Av. Because the first words of the Haftarah from the prophet Isaiah are "Console, console [*nachamu, nachamu*] My people, says your God," this Shabbat is called *Shabbat Nachamu*. Isaiah is assuring the Jews that despite the destruction of the Temple, God has not forgotten His people. He will comfort the children of Israel. In this Torah reading Moses also has words of comfort and an important warning.

The Parashah begins with Moses' explanation to the Israelites: "I pleaded – [*va-etchannan,* the name of the Parashah] – with the Lord," meaning that Moses pleaded to be allowed to enter the Promised Land with his people. God refused. Moses accepts God's judgment and explains that Joshua, a man of proven abilities, will take his place. All will be well with Israel if they obey the commandments and follow their new leader. He then reminds them about the laws that they must not add to or subtract from, and for the first time they hear the *Sh'ma* [*Sh'ma Yisrael Adonai Eloheinu Adonai Echad* – Hear oh Israel, the Lord our God, the Lord is One.]. In a very brief statement Moses also forbids them to worship the heavenly bodies: "And when you look up to the sky and behold the sun and the moon and the stars, the whole heavenly host, you must not be lured into bowing down to them or serving them. These the Lord your God allotted to other peoples…." (Deut 4:19) In short, Moses is warning the Israelites about astrology, which some people believe is an important source of information and predictions.

At some point in time all peoples have perceived a connection between the heavenly bodies and their personal lives. The sun provides warmth and light; it permits crops to grow. The moon lights the night and controls the sea tides. Eclipses darken the sun; comets brighten the sky; planets move; different events take place on earth. It is tempting to see a cause and effect relationship between the movement of celestial bodies and individual lives. Astrologers believe that the planets and stars determine human affairs. Particularly important for them is the position of the planets at the time of one's birth. Why should Moses worry that the Israelites might worship the heavenly bodies? He has previously warned them not to worship the idols of the Canaanites; in this Parashah he is implicitly warning them about the astrology of the Chaldeans and others such as the Persians and Greeks whom they will meet later.

Chaldeans lived in Ur, the region in southern Mesopotamia where Abraham was born. They were great experts in astrology, and imposed their ideas on the Babylonian Empire which in the 6th century BCE conquered Judah, destroyed the Temple on the 9th of Av and took the Jews into exile. The king of Babylon, who was himself a Chaldean, ordered that a select group of Jewish young people study "the writings and language of the Chaldeans," (Dan 1:4) meaning that they would study astrology among other subjects. Daniel was one of those young people.

The text of the Book of Daniel tells us that with God's help Daniel and his Jewish friends proved themselves more skilled at prediction than the king's astrologers. (Dan 1:20)

In the Talmud we read that the Almighty regretted that He created the Chaldeans. (Sukkah 52b) Nonetheless some sages of the Talmud refer to certain people – probably the Chaldeans, the Persians and Greeks - being "under planetary influence." (Shabbath 156a) The rabbis struggled with the issue of the possible influence of the planets with one group saying "Israel is immune from planetary influence." (Shabbath 156b) But, when they said that prayer mitigates the effects of the planets, (Shabbath 156b, ftn. 7) they implied that planets had influence over human life.

Many references indicate that the Jews of Talmudic times were at the very least interested in astrology. The interest seemed to increase with time. One proof is that in the 6th century C.E. Jews put a Zodiac on the floor of their synagogue in Beit Alpha in northern Israel. The Jews took the Zodiac from the Greeks, and they gave it the name *mazalot*, plural of the Hebrew word *mazal*. I shall return to this word in a moment.

In post Talmudic times there were famous Jewish experts on the Zodiac and astrology. For example, Masha'allah lived at the end of the 8th century and beginning of the 9th century. Goldstein has written that "Masha'allah was one of the principlal authorities in astrological matters for Muslims, Jews, and Christians in the Middle Ages." (Goldstein, 2001, p. 24)

Rabbi Abraham Ibn Ezra (1089 to 1164) translated works of Masha'allah from Arabic into Hebrew. We know Ibn Ezra today for his brilliant commentaries on Torah and for his many translations into Hebrew of Arab and Indian texts – including texts about astrology and mathematics. His works provide a link between the Muslim and Hindu east and the Jewish and Christian west. He also wrote his own astrological treatises including the "Book of Selections" which "tells the various positions of the stars which [predict] the fate of every [person] at the moment of his [or her] birth, and the choice of the celestial influences under which one might advantageously undertake certain enterprises." (Levy, p. 13) This great scholar had more than an intellectual interest in astrology.

Saadia Gaon, who was a more influential scholar and teacher, wrote *The Book of Beliefs and Opinions* in about 933. It has been called "the first systematic presentation of Judaism as a rational body of beliefs." (Rosenblatt, p. xxiv) In his position as Gaon, head of the Jewish Talmudic Academy, he had great prestige in the Jewish world. Although he dismissed claims that the so-called ascendant planet at the time of one's birth influenced a person for the rest of his or her life, he legitimized "the study of both astronomy and astrology in the context of a religiously significant work." (Goldstein, 2001, p. 40) Documents found in the Cairo Geniza show that Jews of the 10th and 11th centuries often prepared the horoscope of a newborn child. (Goitein, Vol. III, p. 233) They were certainly trying to understand the influence of the planets on that child.

The Hebrew word for planet is *mazal.* According to Moshe Idel, the great scholar of mysticism, "In ancient Hebrew, the word mazzal…used in the context of the twelve signs of the zodiac, has a variety of meanings, ranging from 'luck' or 'fortune' on the one hand, to the individual [zodiac] signs, on the other. In this last sense, it denotes a complex structure or constellation of …stars [seen] as a source of influences [on] each individual in accordance with the moment of his or her birth." (Idel, p. 20)

Today when Jews want to congratulate someone on the birth of a child, a marriage, graduation from college, they say *"mazal tov."* The literal sense of this expression is "may your planet or constellation be good" or "may the stars treat you well." In other words, by saying *"mazal tov"* one is implicitly making reference to the stars and astrology.

How can we reconcile this common expression, *mazal tov,* with Moses' warning in this week's Parashah not to "bow down to the sun, the moon, the stars and the heavenly host."? Like the pious Jews of the Middle Ages, who could quote horoscope as well as scripture, Jews today could find a way around the contradiction by saying that God, creator of heaven and earth, controls the celestial bodies.

The vast majority of Jews today doubt the influence of the stars and planets over daily life, careers, and choice of spouse. One can, however, forgive someone for hoping for a little good luck or *mazal* from time to time.

# 46

## *Eikev*

◆

## *(Deuteronomy 7:12 – 11:25)*

In the last Parashah Moses repeated the Ten Commandments. In Parashat *Eikev* he orders the Israelites to obey: "And if [*eikev*] you do obey these rules and observe them carefully, the Lord your God will maintain faithfully for you the covenant…. He will favor you and bless you and multiply you…." (Deut 7:12-13). God will protect you against the other nations and will remove them from your path. To remember God's words God told us in Parashat *Va-etchannan* to "bind them as a sign on your hand and let them serve as a symbol on your forehead, and teach them to your children…and inscribe them on the doorposts of your house and on your gates."(Deut 6:8-9) Wearing *tefillin* and putting *mezuzot* on the entrances through which we pass will help us to remember and then to obey.

Moses explains, as he did many times, that God is particularly concerned that the Israelites will fall victim to the idols and the idolatry of the peoples whom they meet. Therefore, the instructions are to burn the idols when you see them; do not take any into your house. Moses admits that God tests His people in order to know whether or not they will remain faithful to Him. Maybe the greatest test will be when they are comfortably settled in their own land. Perhaps they will forget the One who freed them from slavery; perhaps they will think one god is as good as any other and turn to the idols. If they do, they will perish.

As a consequence of their victories, the Israelites might mistakenly think they were chosen by the Almighty because of some imagined superiority to other peoples, that they are more virtuous by nature than others. Moses disabuses them of these false notions concerning their status as Chosen People: "it is rather because of the wickedness of those nations that the Lord is dispossessing them…. It is not because of your virtues and your rectitude….." In fact, Moses continues, "you are a stiff-necked people. You are defiant."

(Deut. 9:4-7) Recalling their sins, he says: You made an idol, the golden calf. Frequently you have lost faith in God. (Deut 9:12)

The Israelites are frail human beings subject to many temptations; they are basically no better than anyone else, but once God chose them to worship God and to carry the message of God's oneness and power to the world, God was reluctant to dispense with them and to choose someone else. According to Moses, the second reason for God's choice is because of promises made to Abraham, Isaac and Jacob who were loyal and obedient to God even though they were not perfect. These ancestors and other leaders preserved the Covenant with God by showing God their loyalty.

Abraham left his home to travel to an unknown land; he was willing to sacrifice his son. Isaac was ready to die. Sarah suffered abuse to save her husband and the Covenant. Rebekah understood God's choice of Jacob. Jacob struggled with God's emissary but obeyed. Joseph suffered as a slave until he could save Egypt and Israel from famine. Judah understood repentance. Moses gave up the comforts of a princely life to lead an oppressed people to freedom. The prophets all obeyed – even Jonah eventually. Collectively their actions saved Israel from God's wrath.

These men and women give us hope that, as weak as we may be, we can strive for ways to obey God's will, to affirm the Covenant, and to prove in our own small ways that God did make the right choice.

# 47

## *R'eih*

✦

### *(Deuteronomy 11:26 - 16:17)*

In this Parashah, Moses wants to emphasize in very simple terms the choices the Israelites must make. He begins: "See [*r'eih* - the name of the Parashah] this day I set before you blessing and curse, blessing, if you obey the commandments of the Lord your God..., and curse if you do not obey the commandments of the Lord your God, but turn away from the path that I enjoin upon this day and follow other gods, whom you have not experienced." (Deut 11:26-28) To ensure that the Israelites avoid the temptation of the Canaanite idols when they cross over into the Promised Land, Moses orders them to "[t]ear down their altars, smash their pillars, put their sacred posts to the fire, and cut down the images of their gods, obliterating their name from that site." (Deut 12:3) Two questions arise from these admonitions: What's wrong with making images of gods? What's wrong with making an image representing the One and Only God?

The first question is easy to answer. God says that you will be cursed if you "follow other gods, whom you have not experienced." In other words, for forty years you have benefited from the devotion and power of the One God. He saved you from slavery; fed you in the desert; gave you the law; defeated your enemies, and is about to bring you into your new land. Turning to idols would be an egregious act of ingratitude. Furthermore, worshipping idols is a waste of time. The Hebrew word for "image" or "idol" in this Parashah is *fesel*, the same as in the Ten Commandments. Cognates of this word, based on the same three-consonant root are *psolet* meaning "worthless matter" and *pasul* meaning "defective" or "disqualified."(Schaechter-Haham, p. 534) In other words, don't waste your time with false, useless gods, and be grateful that you have been chosen.

Second, why are we forbidden to make images of the One and Only God? To make an idol is to reduce God to an object which we have created in a form we choose. Such an action would be supremely arrogant. A material object can be moved, ignored, soiled, and destroyed. In short, making an idol is akin to denying God's power and is an implicit assertion of our own power, worse than the project to build the Tower of Babel. One might respond that the idol is not really God; rather, it reminds us of God. This, too, is difficult to believe because once the idol is made people easily slip into worship of the visible, palpable object.

We know that people crave visible signs of God's presence and God's power. Even praying at the *Kotel*, the Western Wall in Jerusalem, the only remnant of the second Temple, may lead some to worshipping an object.

After the destruction of the Temple Jews had little to look at in order to remind them of the presence of God. In the 3rd century of the Common Era Jews painted beautiful frescoes showing Abraham, Esther and other biblical figures in their Dura Europos Synagogue in present-day Syria, but that example is very rare. We have nothing that approaches the paintings and statues of other religions which are often amazingly beautiful. It is true we have symbols such as the eternal light, the *ner tamid*, in houses of worship, but they are reminders of what our ancestors were ordered to put into the Temple. The most important image is the simple message above arks in many synagogues, namely, "Know before whom you stand."

Knowing God means studying God's words in the Torah. Studying the Torah means trying to obey the commandments. We approach God directly without visual objects other than His words written in the Torah and the words of the sages in the Talmud. We must live with an abstraction, an idea of the Almighty. In short, Judaism is a profoundly intellectual religion.

# 48

## *Shof'tim*

✦

### *(Deuteronomy 16:18-21:9)*

In previous Parashot we have read about priests and prophets, but where is the secular authority which will govern the Israelites and settle daily disputes? In this Parashah Moses tells the Israelites that God wants them to have judges for their government. "You shall appoint magistrates [*shof'tim,* the name of the Parashah] and officials [*shotrim*] for your tribes....and they shall govern the people with due justice. [The judges] will not judge unfairly; you shall show no partiality; you shall not take bribes." (Deut 16:19) "Justice, justice shall you pursue, that you may thrive and occupy the land that the Lord your God is giving you." (Deut 16:20)

Rashi emphasizes the importance of judges for Israel's future: "The appointment of honest judges is sufficient merit to keep Israel in life and to settle them in security in their land." (Rashi on Deut 16:20)

Judges did more than settle disputes. Between the death of Joshua, who succeeded Moses, and the appointment of Saul as king several generations of judges guided Israel. The Book of Judges is the best source of information about them. They governed in a broad sense and led the defense of the community as well as settled disputes within the community. The verb *shafat* means to judge, to decide, to govern, and to administer justice. (Schaechter-Hamam, p. 722) We read about judges leading the Israelites in battle against external enemies such as the Canaanites and helping consolidate Israelite occupation of the Promised Land.

One famous judge was Deborah (Judges 4:4). We read about this woman in various sources. One says she belonged to the tribe of Naphtali. (Yalkut HaMechiri, cited by Chasidah, p. 128); another explains that she was rich. (*Targum Shoftim* 4:5, cited by Chasidah, p. 128). In the Book of Judges (4:5) we read that she was known as the judge who sat under a palm tree while weighing arguments and making decisions. A reason for that may have been her concern that no one think she met privately with men she was not related to. (Chasidah, p. 128)

When the Canaanites, led by Sisera, the military commander, threatened Israel, Deborah took the initiative to attack him. She named a man, Barak, to be her military commander; she planned the strategy, and the Israelites won the victory.

The reactions to Deborah as a woman leader are contradictory. Rabbi Nahman (Megillah 14b) was notably irked by her initiatives, particularly by her summoning of Barak. She should have gone to see Barak rather than summoning him, the rabbi reasoned. Rabbi Nahman further claimed her name means "hornet" and that she was haughty, which does not, he added, "befit women." Other rabbis praise Deborah as a person who restored Israel's strength and devotion to God. (Zohar, *Bereshith*, I:32b) These rabbis implicitly make fun of Rabbi Nahman "There is a dictum: Woe to the man at whose table the wife says grace. So when we read that 'Deborah judged Israel at that time' we might say: 'Woe to the generation which could only find a female to be its judge.'" These rabbis praise Deborah for her skills which included singing and poetry. According to Zohar, "there were two women in the world who composed praises to God such as the men never equaled, namely Hannah and Deborah…." (Zohar *Vayikra*, III: 19b)

These rabbis respected the contribution of particular women. It is unlikely they would have generalized to all women. Today, however, we understand that our community is most just and most strong when men and women participate fully and equally in all aspects of Jewish life.

# 49

## Ki Tetzei

✦

## (Deuteronomy 21:10 -25:19)

Capital punishment is the authorized killing of a person deemed a threat to his or her society. Despite the many commandments and instructions in the Torah to kill evil doers, the Israelites and the post-Biblical Jews down to the present have opposed the death penalty in practice. Why?

### Capital Punishment In Torah

In Numbers 35:31 it is written that if a person is properly convicted of murder, a capital crime, "he must be put to death." Not even a ransom can save him. There are many other cases of capital crimes. We read in Parashat *Ki Tetzei* that the parents of a son who is "wayward and defiant" who is "disloyal," "a glutton and a drunkard" are supposed to bring him to the town elders who "shall stone him to death." (Deut 21:18-21) He did not kill anyone, but Maimonides' disturbing explanation is that he is to be executed "on account of what he might become, because he will likely be a murderer..." (Maimonides, p. 346) According to one count, there are 35 other capital crimes in Torah (Mendelsohn, pp. 44-45); they include desecration of the Sabbath, idolatry, blasphemy, sorcery, various sexual transgressions as well as murder. The crimes seem unambiguous and the punishment crystal clear.

Stoning is the preferred form of execution. Witnesses to the crime and others throw rocks at the condemned person. The guilty party could also be pushed off the edge of a cliff. Stoning is also a metaphor for punishment when the prophet Ezekiel predicts that an unfaithful Israel will be stoned. (Ezekiel 23:47). Other means of execution are burning, strangulation and beheading. These four forms of capital punishment are to be used after proper deliberations – notably a trial before the Sanhedrin.

The Great Sanhedrin or supreme court or council existed while the Temple existed; it consisted of 71 pious and respected men. Their authority was based on the idea that they were the successors through the centuries of the original elders chosen by Moses. It was understood that "the divine spirit that [had] been bestowed on Moses [would] now also rest on the elders." (Milgrom, pp. 86-87, note 16) This council also served as an advisory and legislative council. "[F]rom the time of the Hasmoneans onward [in the second century BCE]" it determined capital punishment. (Alon, p. 203) According to Alon, smaller councils outside Jerusalem had authority, but, unlike the town elders in this Parashah, they probably did not have in practice the authority to condemn a person to death.

Rules in the Torah guided the deliberations of the Sanhedrin: There had to be two or three witnesses for a capital conviction (Deut 17:6), and witnesses had to participate in the execution of the guilty party.(Deut 17:7) The latter requirement must have given pause to people thinking about accusing someone else of a capital crime.

No trial by the Sanhedrin was necessary for persons caught desecrating the Temple area or stealing from the Temple. Guardians of the Temple would dispatch them immediately. (Segal, p. 51)

## Rabbinic Commentary

As rabbis interpreted the meaning of Torah they added hurdles to the imposition of capital punishment. They established procedures limiting its application. For example, they said witnesses should be "intimidated" meaning that they must be questioned in great detail about what they claimed they saw or heard; judges had to remind them about the risks of mistake; circumstantial evidence was discounted (Sanhedrin 37a) They added safeguards for the accused. For example, a person who was ignorant of the law and was not informed about the punishment for breaking the law could not be condemned to death. (Cf Neusner, *The Tosefta*, Vol. I, Shabbat 8:5, p. 382). They said the Sanhedrin may impose the death penalty only as long as the priests were performing their duties in the Temple. (Sanhedrin 52b, Bleich, pp.111-112)

Because of the destruction of the Temple and the two Jewish wars with the Romans, which led to a great disruption in Jewish society, the Sanhedrin could no longer impose the death penalty. The institution lost its authority. More interesting is the opposition to the death penalty on principle.

Rabbi Akiba (50-135 CE) vigorously opposed the death penalty on principle; he and his colleague Rabbi Tarfon said: "If we had been members of the Sanhedrin no man would have ever been put to death." Rabbi Akiba dismissed the case of the rebellious son that I mentioned from this Parashah, saying "there has never been, and there never will be, a rebellious and incorrigible son. So why has the passage been written?" His own answer was that we are to study God's instructions for the sake of study. We shall learn some lessons and be rewarded thereby. Akiba also reportedly said "Whoever spills blood destroys the image (of God)…" (Blidstein, p.320, Cf. Sanhedrin in Neusner, *The Tosefta*, pp. 1143-1197) Other rabbis said in the Mishnah that if the Sanhedrin had ordered the killing of a convicted murderer once in seven years, that would be too frequent. (Makkot 1:10) They said they believed saving one life is like saving "a complete world" and that killing one life is like "destroying a complete world." (Sanhedrin 37a) Certainly some rabbis supported capital punishment, but Urbach says that Rabbis Akiba and Tarfon "reflected a trend and an outlook in accord with the historical reality of their time." (Urbach, *Halakhah*, p. 71)

Finally, rabbis provided the perfect solution for both the opponents and supporters of the death penalty. Humans need not decide capital cases at all. If God decreed death for certain crimes such as murder and idolatry, it is God who will take the life of the guilty party. Thus, the person who would have been stoned will fall off a roof; the person who would have been burned is bitten by a snake; the person who would have been sentenced to decapitation is killed by the Romans; and the person who during the time of the Sanhedrin would have been strangled drowns. (Sanhedrin 37b and see ftn. 9)

## The Death Penalty In The State of Israel

Israel inherited the death penalty from the British Mandate, but rabbinic authorities opposed capital punishment for murder. Since the State of Israel did not explicitly incorporate *Halakhah* into statutory law, other capital crimes such as desecration of the Sabbath and idolatry were moot. Debates in the Israeli legislature or Knesset show that Members of the Knesset were well aware of rabbinic sentiment in the Talmud and used it to oppose the death penalty.

In 1954 the government of Israel offered a statute for the repeal of the death penalty for murder but not for genocide. Law minister Rosen who presented the proposed law to the Knesset based the government's reasoning on the Torah, the Talmud and modern secular values. He said that although Torah mandates death for a number of infractions of the law, the sages "constructed fences….in the process of trial and judgment" making application very difficult. Then, basing his remarks on the Talmud, the minister said that after the destruction of the Second Temple and the end of the Sanhedrin, "there is no authority" to issue the death penalty and "in the course of time, the

death penalty has become alien to the spirit of the nation in the Diaspora…"
(P. Rosen in Rakover, p. 517) The maximum penalty is "separation from the
community…." by which he meant prison.

The minister's main argument for abolition was more secular, namely,
the possibility of judicial mistakes and the subsequent execution of innocent
persons. Orthodox MKs (Members of the Knesset) such as Mr. Verhaftig
vigorously supported the proposed abolition: "Our laws are not the commands
of God, and therefore we have no right to take the life of a man which is in
the hands of God." (Rakover, p. 518) A court's decision to execute someone
is, therefore, judicial murder. The repeal of the death penalty "will be an
educational means to increase the value of human life." Another Member
of the Knesset said that imprisonment with its consequent humiliation is
a better deterrent to murder than is capital punishment. In any case, "The
death penalty is foreign to the spirit of Judaism…,"one MK added. (Rakover,
p.526) Yet another argued that in Jewish tradition there is the possibility of
atonement, but in secular law it does not exist. The MK said that without the
possibility of atonement, there can be no death penalty. (Rakover, p. 535).

The bill passed the Knesset and the law (Abolition of Death Penalty for
Murder Law, 5714 – 1954) dated 16th February 1954 now reads: "Where a
person has been convicted of murder, the Court shall impose the penalty of
imprisonment for life, and only that penalty…." The law specifies, however,
that the death penalty is valid punishment for war crimes which include
killing hostages and general crimes against humanity and the Jewish people.
(Baker, p. 57) The State of Israel applied capital punishment to the Nazi mass
murderer Adolph Eichmann in 1962.

As a result of Israel's law and practice, Amnesty International puts
Israel among "117 countries which have abolished the death penalty in law
or practice." (Amnesty International) The sentiment against a judicially
sanctioned death penalty is so strong that the Knesset passed another law
forbidding Israel from extraditing a person to another country if that person
may be subject to the death penalty there. (Baker, p. 124)

We see that in Jewish law and tradition opposition to the death penalty
depends in part on procedural issues: are there enough witnesses; is there
a qualified judicial body to take a human life, was the miscreant warned.
Prophets and sages from Talmudic times and the Israeli government of the
20th century oppose the death penalty also on principle despite the dozens of
orders in Torah to inflict the death penalty. According to the prophet Ezekiel,
this opposition is not in violation of *Halakhah*. Speaking on behalf of God
the prophet said, "It is not My desire that the wicked shall die, but that the
wicked turn from [their] ways and live." (Ezekiel 33:11) In other words, the

worst criminals should have the opportunity to repent even if they must do it while spending the rest of their lives in prison.

So, what is the answer to my question about the basic reasons for ancient and modern Jewish opposition to the death penalty? The answer comes from the Torah, of course. Although the Almighty harangues us many times about crime and threatens us with death and exile, He consistently offers the possibility of repentance, atonement and forgiveness. During the month of Elul when we read this particular Parashah Jews are preparing for the Ten Days of Awe, Rosh Hashanah through Yom Kippur, during which everyone consciously engages in repentance. In this time of self-assessment Jews are to remember among other things one strong and enduring message related to the subject of capital punishment. God's message is stated most explicitly in Parashat *Nitzavim* (Deut 29:9-30:20). Two simple words from this Parashah (Deut 30:19) provide the answer to my question, two words which, in my opinion, are an important message Jews carry to the rest of the world: "**Choose Life**."

# 50

## *Ki Tavo*

✦

### *(Deuteronomy. 26 - 29:8)*

The Israelites are now very close to the Promised Land, and Moses gives them specific last-minute instructions: "When you enter the land" which, in Hebrew, is *Ki tavo el Ha-Aretz* – the name of the Parashah - and begin to cultivate the soil, you will give the first fruits to the priests for an offering. As you do this you must make a series of affirmations, beginning with: "I acknowledge this day before the Lord...that I have entered the land that the Lord swore to our fathers to assign us." (Deut 26:3) Moses then demands more specific affirmations.

On the other side of the river, the Israelites will divide themselves into two parts, half will climb one mountain, and half will climb the opposite mountain. The Levites will stand in the valley between them and will proclaim a series of curses and blessings such as: "Cursed be anyone who makes a sculpted or molten image…." Although the word "amen" is said very frequently during daily prayers, "amen" which means "so be it" and also "faith" occurs rarely in the Torah. It is mainly in this Parashah that one reads "amen." What is the significance of answering "amen" here?

Until the moment the Israelites cross the Jordan, their acceptance of the commandments has been implicit. Of course, they had to obey and were punished for not obeying, but they did not have to "sign on the dotted line," so to speak. In our Parashah, the Lord is asking for a positive, active commitment to the covenant, and, as in most contracts, the parties must accept the consequences for non-compliance. Action is crucial for compliance and non-compliance.

In Judaism, we are judged for actions and failure to act. According to Menachem Kellner, "each one of us is born pure; it is our job in living to remain pure…. But no matter how bad a mess one makes of one's life, the doctrine of repentance teaches that God is always available to the *ba'al teshuvah*, the repentant individual." (Kellner, p. 45)

During the month of Elul, prior to the High Holy Days, Jews think about repentance for having violated provisions of the Covenant. The holy texts and scholars remind Jews that we are party to the original Covenant. Rabbi Joseph Soloveitchik wrote: "every act of repentance required official acceptance and a sworn commitment by the 'persona" which is tantamount to re-enactment of a covenant between the Holy One, blessed be He, and the sinner." (Cited by Peli, p. 218) The repetition of the word "amen" in this week's Parashah seems time-based, but our ancestors were also speaking for us. In the next Parashah we read: "I [God] make this covenant with its sanctions not with you alone, but with those who are not with us here this day...." meaning future generations (Deut 29:13-14).

The time gap between Jews of today and the Israelites that we read about in this Parashah is great; today the political, ritual and cultural gap between us and other Jews living who do not share our secular and religious concerns is also great, if not greater. But, remember one thing: when Jews all over the world read the explicit affirmations of agreement with the Covenant, and when we ourselves say "amen," during the Torah reading and in our prayers, we are united with all Jews over space and over time.

# 51

## *Nitzavim*

✦

## *(Deuteronomy 29:9 – 30:20)*

This week's Parashah begins with the words, "you are standing before the Lord," *atem nitzavim hayom kulchem lifnei Adonai. Nitsavim* is "standing" in the sense of presenting yourselves. (*Etz Hayim,* 29:9) Moses means that the Israelites present themselves in order to "enter into the covenant" or to renew the Covenant with the Almighty. It is not sufficient that their ancestors agreed to the Covenant; every generation must affirm their agreement to the terms, and that includes those who are here now and those to come in the future. If they decide to disobey, they will be punished; if they decide to obey – even after initially disobeying – God will ensure their survival and happiness. The choice is clear: "See, I set before you this day life and prosperity, death and adversity." (Deut 30:15) "I have put before you life and death, blessing and curse. Choose life…by loving the Lord your God, heeding His commands and holding fast to Him." (Deut 30:19-20)

Joshua will repeat these words after the Israelites have crossed the River Jordan into the Promised Land, saying "if you are loath to serve the Lord choose this day which ones you are going to serve…" The people respond that they will serve the one and only Almighty God, and Joshua responds "You are witnesses against yourselves that you have by your own act chosen to serve the Lord." (Josh 24:22) We can hear the word "choose" echoing in the Judean hills. God and Moses constantly tell us we have free will.

We might be tempted to respond that it is God who has free choice, not us. God chose us to serve Him even though we had no particular merit. We were never better than anyone else, Moses says. God chose our homeland, and God chose the terms of the Covenant without consulting us. I looked but can find no reference to a constitutional referendum in the Bible.

True, but it is amazing the number of free choices made by individuals – Jews and non-Jews - that we read about in Tanakh. Abraham did not have to obey God; he willingly left his homeland and he willingly almost killed his son. Judah changed himself from a jealous brother into a leader of his family. Moses chose loyalty to his people and signaled to God his leadership capabilities when he killed the Egyptian foreman abusing an Israelite. Job chose to suffer rather than renounce the Lord; Hanna chose to dedicate her son Samuel to the Lord's service. Ruth honored her mother-in-law (Torah only tells us to honor our parents, not the in-laws.) Then, Ruth willingly joined her life with Israel. Bad people also have free will. Absalom chose to revolt. Amalekites gratuitously attacked Israel; Haman decided to kill the Jews.

Recognizing we have free will means we cannot blame others for our mistakes.

We Jews are taught to take responsibility for the errors we have committed against God and against our fellow human beings, Jews and non-Jews. With God's commandments as our guide, God grants us a chance to repent and then to correct ourselves which is what we try to achieve in the days before Rosh Hashanah when this Parashah is read and studied. We thank God we can know what is right and what is wrong even if we often fail to choose to follow the high standards of His teaching.

When the question about human freedom arises, I agree with Isaac Bashevis Singer. During a television appearance after the Nobel Prize announcement Singer was asked if he believed in free will. He replied: "Of course I believe in free will; I have no choice."

# 52

## *Va-yeilekh*

✦

## *(Deuteronomy 31:1-31:30*

In a Bible quiz one might answer the following question with the names of different biblical persons:

1. Who led the Israelites through a body of water that miraculously parted; then sent spies to survey the Promised Land; wrote down our laws? Answer: Moses.
2. Which leader defeated the enemies of Israel on the battlefield? Answer: David.
3. Which ancestor was completely faithful to another, going wherever that person went and helping selflessly in all ways? Answer: Ruth.
4. The Almighty changed whose name as they took on a new role? Answer: Abraham, Sarah, Jacob, and Joshua.
5. Whom did God command to circumcise all males as a Covenant obligation? Answer: Abraham.

All are correct, but the single answer to all the above questions would be Joshua the son of Nun, who succeeded Moses.

In this Parashah, Moses "in the sight of all Israel" charged Joshua to become the leader "who shall go with this people into the land…and it is [he] who shall apportion it to them." (Deut 31:7) Now the Israelites are poised to conquer their land, and in the fourteen years to come Joshua would bring to fruition God's command and promise to Abraham: "Go forth from your native land and from your father's house to the land that I will show you." (Gen 12:1) "I will assign this land to your offspring." (Gen 12:7)

Joshua seems to be a model of perfection. What does Torah tell us about him? What does the Book of Joshua tell us about him? What does his life teach us about obedience, sin and repentance, topics very much on our minds as Rosh Hashanah and Yom Kippur approach.

# Joshua in the Torah

The Torah tells us that Joshua belonged to the tribe of Ephraim, descendants of Joseph's younger son. He was born a slave in Egypt, the son of Nun, and named Hosea. He showed his military prowess early in the history of the Exodus when he "overwhelmed the people of Amalek with the sword." (Ex 17:14) Joshua was Moses' confidant and attendant when Moses ascended Mt. Sinai to receive the Law. He accompanied Moses to the Tent of Meeting and stayed there in God's presence after Moses went out.

Moses appointed him as one of the twelve spies on a mission to reconnoiter the Land of Canaan and changed his name from Hosea to Joshua before he left on his mission.(Num 13:16) Why the change of name? Hosea, *hei-vav-shin-ayin,* means "salvation," "help," or possibly "helper." By adding the letter *yod* making his name *yod- hei- vav-shin-ayin* or "Yehoshua" which we read as "Joshua," the meaning changes to "God saves" or "God helps," or possibly "May God save you." (Sotah 34b)

Why change his name before his mission to search out the land and not earlier before the battle with the Amalekites? The reason is that the threat of doubt – in the form of self-doubt and in the form of doubting God's will and commandments – is greater than any human threat to the Israelites. Joshua will need God's protection from doubt and fear on the mission. (The association of the name Joshua with saving is so powerful that in Christian belief Joseph is instructed to call his wife Mary's son Joshua which, according to the Gospel of Matthew, means "he will save his people from their sins." (Matthew 1:21) The Greek form of this name is, of course, Jesus.)

Joshua bin Nun, along with Caleb is saved from doubt, and unlike the other spies, he survives the 40-year trek, reaching the age of 96 by the time of Moses' death. It is Joshua who completed the Book of Deuteronomy by writing about Moses' death. He also went on to write the Book of Joshua with the exception of the last verses describing his own death.

# Joshua in the Book of Joshua

At the beginning of this book the Lord appeared to Joshua and promised the same support in crossing the River Jordan and taking the Promised Land that He had previously given to Moses in the Exodus from Egypt.

Joshua sent two spies to Jericho. They met Rahab, possibly a prostitute, living in that city. She gave the spies useful information and hid them in her house. The spies returned safely, and unlike the spies that Moses sent, they gave a favorable report. Joshua then ordered the people to advance toward the river.

The Ark of the Covenant was carried to the river's edge by the priests. As the priests moved into the water a pathway miraculously appeared, and the Israelites walked over dry land to the other side. They set up their camp within the Promised Land where Joshua circumcised the males because none has been circumcised during the past 40 years trek through the desert. The Israelites then celebrated Passover; manna ceased to appear; and the people nourished themselves with food from the land. Suddenly, Joshua experienced a vision (Josh 5:13) which the sages interpreted as a warning that he had been neglecting the study of Torah and the offering of sacrifices at the mobile altar. (Eiruvin 63b) I shall return to this warning below.

Joshua pressed on with his military actions. His troops conquered Jericho, and in gratitude, according to tradition, he composed the *Aleinu* prayer. According to the Talmud (Megilah 14b), Joshua found Rahab, who had been so helpful to the spies, and after she converted, he married her. In the course of time, according to tradition, she gave birth to daughters.

The battles resumed with the attempted conquest of the city of Ai where the Israelite troops failed because one Israelite had stolen gold and silver at Jericho that was supposed to be offered to God at the Sanctuary. Responding to Joshua's pleas, God allowed the conquest to continue. Joshua built an altar and made the required sacrifices. He copied the laws on stones and read the blessings and the curses to all the Israelites assembled on two hills.

The conquest continued for seven years. Even though Joshua had not conquered all of the Promised Land, he ceased hostilities and spent the next seven years dividing the land among the tribes. By the time he completed this task Joshua was 110 years old; he knew he would soon die. In his farewell address Joshua told the Israelites that one day they would possess all of the land from the river to the Great Sea; they must keep the commandments; if they worshipped false gods, the One and True God would punish them. He reminded them of their history and their ancestors beginning with Abraham, father of all Israel. He asked them to affirm voluntarily their adherence to the Covenant. All Israel promised to serve the Lord. (Joshua 24:21) Joshua then died. (Josh 24:29). After his death and burial, the Israelites also buried the bones of Joseph at Shechem.

The return of Joseph's bones to Israel closed the circle. Joseph had taken the Israelites to Egypt, and Joseph's descendant Joshua took the Israelites back home. According to Midrash, Moses selected Joshua to lead the battle against Amalek because he was a descendant of Joseph. (*Pesikta Rabbati,* Piska 12. "Summary," p. 216)

The story of the Israelites might have ended with the Book of Joshua. Finally, they had reached the land God promised their ancestor Abraham. What else is there to tell?

God would send other prophets to tell Israel of its sins. If a man such as Joshua could sin, so could all of Israel.

## Lessons from Joshua's Alleged Sins

According to Talmud, sins such as the Golden Calf necessitate the rebukes and harangues we read in the books of the prophets, the psalms and proverbs. (Nedarim 22b). But, what about Joshua?

It is difficult to believe that a hero such as Joshua could be accused of any failings or sins, but, as the Talmud tells us, Joshua was criticized for neglecting the study of Torah and for failing to oversee the sacrifices. These omissions seem minor because he was busy leading the Israelites in battle. Nonetheless, his punishment was severe since, according to tradition, he and Rahab had no sons. (Sotah 35a) If Joshua could not be perfect, who is capable of being perfect according to the Almighty? One concludes that imperfection, not perfection is part of God's plan for us.

In Parashat *Va-yeilekh* Moses predicted that the Israelites would make mistakes and would disobey God in one way or another: "I know that, when I am dead, you will act wickedly and turn away from the path that I enjoined upon you, and that in time to come misfortune will befall you...." (Deut 31:29)

God tells us to obey the Commandments. God expects at least partial failure, but is always ready to forgive if Israel repents. According to one very beautiful Midrash, Satan loads one side of a scale with Israelite iniquities while God loads the other side of the scale with Israel's good deeds. One side is in perfect balance with the other. Satan rushes off to find more sins in order to tilt the scale, but in Satan's absence God removes some of the sins and hides them. Satan returns and sees the scale tipping toward just deeds and obedience; he complains angrily to God: "Master of the Universe, You have carried away the iniquity of Your people." (*Pesikta Rabbati*, Piska 45, Summary 2, pp.783-784 commenting on Psalm 85:3)

We know that God wants Jews to repent for all the errors in order that He may redeem His people. He will not allow a return to the status quo ante, however. Sins of omission and commission must be forgiven, but individuals' lives must also change. Moses cannot enter the Promised Land; Joshua will have no sons; the Israelites must spend forty years in the desert so that a new generation might emerge which will enter the Promised Land. This is how human history evolves, meaning successes, failures, renewed efforts, and constant struggle to reach goals. Such a view of history may explain why our Torah ends with the fifth book, Deuteronomy, before the Israelites are settled finally in their Promised Land rather than with the Book of Joshua which ends with the successful conquest and settlement of much of the land.

God is saying that our history is incomplete. We always reside on the edge of finality just as our ancestors stopped on the edge of the Promised Land at the end of Deuteronomy. He is telling us that we have not yet lived enough, meaning we have not obeyed enough; we have not sinned enough meaning we have not struggled enough with the temptations of the world around us; we have not repented enough; we have not been forgiven enough. Thus, we continue to participate in an evolving history as individuals and as a community in the years to come.

Only God can decide when history must end. Jeremiah told us God's plan (Jeremiah 50:19-20):

> And I will lead Israel back to his pasture
> In those days and at that time – declares the Lord –
> The iniquity of Israel shall be sought,
> And there shall be none;
> The sins of Judah,
> And none shall be found,
> For I will pardon those I allow to survive.

# 53

## *Ha-azinu*

✦

### *(Deuteronomy 32:1 – 32:52)*

The Sabbath between Rosh HaShanah and Yom Kippur is called *Shabbat Shuvah* after the first words of the Haftarah taken from the prophet Hosea: '*Shuvah Yisra-el*," he says. "Return, o Israel, to the Eternal your God, for you have stumbled in your iniquity." (Hosea 14:2) Hosea tells all of us to return to God because we have disobeyed commandments over the past year. On Yom Kippur, Jews collectively confess these iniquities and pray that the Almighty will accept Jews' repentance. Parashat *Ha-azinu* is read on *Shabbat Shuvah*

*Ha-azinu* is also the penultimate Parashah in the Torah. The end of the cycle of Torah readings is approaching, and so is Moses' life coming to an end. He is fully aware that his death is imminent. He seems alternately depressed and hopeful, worried that Israel will disobey the commandments, but confident that despite our weaknesses, God is ready to forgive and accept us again if we repent.

Moses believes that before he dies he can provide his people with a method in the form of a poem to remember their obligations. Whether we fulfill these obligations or not is, of course, up to us. It is our choice.

The first words of this poem, *Ha-azinu* mean "give ear" or "listen." Moses' words are literally addressed to heaven and earth as witnesses to the Israelites' behavior, but he wants the Israelites to memorize the poem and to teach it to their children as a way of governing their behavior. The first part of the poem is an abbreviated history of Israelite relations with the Lord; then, it explains the Lord's punishment of Israel for disobeying the commandments; third, we read about the Almighty's punishment of Israel's enemies who think mistakenly that Israel will disappear; and lastly we read about the ultimate redemption of Israel by a forgiving God.

One verse in this poem leaps from the pages. "Remember the days of old, Consider the years of ages past; Ask your father, he will inform you, Your elders, they will tell you." (Deuteronomy 32:7) This means that we must talk about Torah with others, more knowledgeable than ourselves. Yes, we must read the teachings of the Almighty alone, by ourselves, but it is good to share our questions and ideas with our contemporaries, particularly the elders, the rabbis, the scholars and friends who study the Torah. Reading and discussing Torah also puts us in the presence of the writings of scholars, rabbis, students, and laypersons who for the last 2,500 years have studied and discussed this holy text. In addition to the Talmud, which is vital and central to Torah study, we have the commentaries of the classic medieval rabbinic scholars and the fruits of modern biblical scholarship. All are increasingly accessible through books and the tools of the CD and the Internet.

After Moses finished reciting the poem he said something else which demands our attention: "Take to heart all the words with which I have warned you this day. Enjoin them upon your children that they may observe faithfully all the terms of this Teaching [Torah]... For this is not a trifling thing for you: it is your very life; through it you shall long endure on the land that you are to possess...." (Deut 32:46-47) In other words, without Torah we cease to exist as a people and we cease to live as conscious, goal directed Jews.

These statements tell us that the Torah is accessible and necessary. No matter who we are or where we are, we can and must study it. We must share our questions and conclusions with others.

Are you ever bored or distracted? Pick up the *Tanakh* and read a chapter. Do you have a quiet half hour during the week? Pick up the book and read. Relax; let the text speak. Something wonderful, interesting, or strange will leap out of it. You can share it with others. If you have more time, you can read a Talmudic or scholarly commentary to understand better. It is an enriching experience, a joyful experience, a step on the path of return to God – *Shuvah*.

# 54

## *V'zot ha-B'rakhah*

✦

## *(Deuteronomy 33:1 – 34:12)*

Shortly before his death, which *seems* to mark the end of the Torah, Moses, who is 120 years old, says farewell by blessing the Israelites. *V'zot ha-b'rakhah,* meaning "this is the blessing." He blesses each tribe beginning with the descendants of Reuben, the first-born of Jacob/Israel:"May Reuben live and not die." Also,"Hearken. O Lord, to the voice of Judah." To the loyal Levites: "smash the loins of those rising up against Him." Benjamin is called "The beloved of the Lord." Joseph: "Blessed by the Lord be his land." Zevulun: "Rejoice, O Zevulun, in your going out." Gad: "like a king of beasts he dwells." Dan "is a whelp of lions." "Naftali is sated with favor;" Asher is the "most blessed of sons" (Deut 33:6-25) After 40 years of haranguing and pushing his followers, Moses' last lecture contains words of love and respect; he prays and predicts

> "And Israel dwelled securely,
> untroubled Jacob's abode,
> in a land of grain and wine,
> its heavens, too, drop dew.
> Happy are you, Israel. Who is like you?
> A people delivered by the Lord."
> (Deut 33:28-29, Alter's translation)

In full view of the children of Israel, Moses then walks alone to the top of Mount Nebo where the Almighty is waiting for him. There, God shows him the Land and tells him that He will fulfill His promise to Abraham, Isaac and Jacob. Moses is no more.

The Israelites mourned him for 30 days, but unlike the reactions of their ancestors to change, this generation was finally strong enough to accept Moses' death without fear of the future. Although there could never be "another prophet in Israel like Moses," (Deut 34:10) the Israelites were prepared for this change. Joshua, already well known for his courage and probity, took the mantle of leadership without any problem. Israel would cross the River Jordan and fulfill God's plan for them.

At the beginning of these remarks, I wrote that this Parashah *seems* to mark the end of Torah. In fact, we recognize there is no end of Torah. This portion is the only one of the 54 Parashot that has no designated Shabbat. It is exclusively read on *Simchat Torah*, no matter on what day of the week this beautiful holy day falls. Immediately after reading the final verse in the 54th Parashah, we begin reading the first verse in the first Parashah, Genesis. We have read that our leader and teacher has died, but we dance and rejoice in the teaching we receive from the mouth of God through the hand of Moses.

God does not want us to dwell on the death of Moses. We respect and love Moses; we honor him, but we do not worship him. In Judaism, there is no cult of the personality. People live and die. Only God is eternal. In our memorial *kaddish* prayer we say nothing about death.

Moses lived; Moses taught us and led us; Moses died. Joshua became our leader and teacher; he too died and was succeeded by others. Like our ancestors we live and study as long as we can before we die. As Rabbi Tarfon said in the *Sayings of the Fathers*, we know we shall never finish, but we cannot stop.

*"When God began to create heaven and earth…."*

(Gen 1:1)

# Sources

Adler, Elkan Nathan (ed.), *Jewish Travellers in the Middle Ages: 19 Firsthand Accounts,* (New York, Dover, 1987), pp. 38-63.

Alon, Gedaliah, *The Jews in Their Land in the Talmudic Age (70 – 640 CE),* trans. and edited by Gershon Levi, (Cambridge, Harvard University Press, 1989).

Alter, Robert, trans and commentary, *The Five Books of Moses,* (New York, Norton, 2004).

Amnesty International, "Facts and figures on the death penalty," ACT 50/008/2004

Baker, Henry, *The Legal System of Israel,* (London, Sweet and Maxwell, 1961).

Bentham, Jeremy, *Defence of Usury,* (London, Routledge, edition of 1992, reprint of 1787 edition).

Biale, David, *Eros and the Jews: From Biblical Israel to Contemporary America,* (Berkeley, University of California, 1997).

Bickerman, Elias, J., *The Jews in the Greek Age,* (Cambridge, Harvard University Press, l988).

Blackburn, Simon, *Lust: The Seven Deadly Sins,* (NewYork, Oxford, 2004).

Bleich, J. David, "Jewish Law and the State's Authority to Punish Crime," in *Cardozo Law Review,* Vol. 12, Feb/Mar 1991, Nos 3 – 4, pp. 829 – 857.

Blenkinsopp, Joseph, "Ahab of Israel and Jehoshaphat of Judah: The Syro-Palestinian Corridor in the Ninth Century," in Jack M. Sasson, editor in chief, *Civilizations of the Ancient Near East,* (Peabody, Mass, Hendrickson, 1995), pp.1309 – 1319.

Blidstein, Gerald, "Capital Punishment – The Classic Jewish Discussion," in Alan Corre (ed), *Understanding the Talmud,* (New York, Ktav, 1975), p. 313 – 324.

Boyarin, Daniel, *Carnal Israel: Reading Sex in Talmudic Culture,* (Berkeley, University of California, 1993).

Brody, Robert, *The Geonim of Babylonia and the Shaping of Medieval Jewish Culture,* (New Haven, Yale University Press, 1998).

Brody, Robert and Herr, Moshe D. (eds.), *Ephraim Urbach: Collected Writings in Jewish Studies,* (Jerusalem: Hebrew University Magnes Press, 1999).

Buckley, Susan L., *Teachings on Usury in Judaism, Christianity and Islam,* Lewiston, The Edwin Mellen Press, 2000.

Cassuto, U., *A Commentary on the Book of Exodus,* trans by Israel Abrahams, (Jerusalem, Magnes, 1997).

*The Call of the Torah,* by Rabbi Elie Munk, E.S. Mazer, Trans, Yitzchok Kirzner, ed, (Brooklyn, Mesorah, 1994).

Chasidah, Yishai, *Encyclopedia of Biblical Personalities,* (Jerusalem, Shaar in conjunction with Mashabim, 1994).

Chavel, Charles B., trans and editor, *Ramban – Commentary on the Torah – Deuteronomy,* (New York, Shilo, 1976).

*Chumash with Targum Onkelos, Haphtaroth and Rashi's Commentary-Bereshith,* trans and annotated by A. M. Silbermann with M. Rosenbaum, (Jerusalem, Silbermann, 5745).

*Chumash with Targum Onkelos, Haphtaroth and Rashi's Commentary – Shemoth,* trans and annotated by A. M. Silbermann with M. Rosenbaum, (Jerusalem, Silbermann, 5745).

*Chumash with Targum Onkelos, Haphtaroth and Rashi's Commentary-Vayikra,* trans and annotated by A. M. Silbermann with M. Rosenbaum, (Jerusalem, Silbermann, 5745).

*Chumash with Targum Onkelos, Haphtaroth and Rashi's Commentary-Bamidbar,* trans and annotated by A. M. Silbermann with M. Rosenbaum, (Jerusalem, Silbermann, 5745).

*Chumash with Targum Onkelos, Haphtaroth and Rashi's Commentary - Devarim,* trans. and annotated by A. M. Silvermann with M. Rosenbaum, (Jerusalem, Silvermann, 5745).

*The Code of Maimonides – Book Thirteen – The Book of Civil Laws,* trans by Jacob J. Rabinowitz, Yale Judaica Series, Vol. II, (New Haven, Yale University Press, 1949).

CNN.com, 22 June 2005.

Cohen, Jeffrey M., "Spies, Princes and Korach's Rebellion," in *Dor le Dor,* X, 4, Summer 1982, pp. 220-228.

Cohen, Shaye J.D., *The Beginnings of Jewishness: Boundaries, Varieties, Uncertainties,* (Berkeley, University of California, 1999).

Cohen Stuart, G.H., *The Struggle in Man between Good and Evil: An Inquiry into the origin of the Rabbinic concept of Yeser Hara,* (Kampen: Uitgeven smaatschappij, J. H. Kok, 1984).

*The Commentators' Bible – Exodus,* ed and trans by Michael Carasik, (Philadelphia, Jewish Publication Society, 2005)

*Daily Prayer Book: Ha-Siddur Ha-Shalem,* trans and annotated by Philip Birnbaum, (New York, Hebrew Publishing Company, 1977).

*Etz Hayim Torah and Commentary*, The Rabbinical Assembly, The United Synagogue of Conservative Judaism, (Philadelphia, The Jewish Publication Society, 1985, 1999).

Feldman, Louis H., *Jew and Gentile in the Ancient World*, (Princeton, Princeton University Press, 1993).

Fox, Everett, trans, introduction, commentary, *The Five Books of Moses*, (New York, Schocken, 1995).

French, Peter A., *The Virtues of Vengeance*, (Lawrence, University of Kansas, 2001).

Gabba, Emilio, "The Social, Economic and Political History of Palestine 63 BCE - CE 70," in W. Horby et al (eds.), *The Cambridge History of Judaism, Vol. Three, The Early Roman Period*, (Cambridge, Cambridge University Press, 1999) pp. 94-168.

Gianotti, Charles R., "The Meaning of the Divine name YHWH," in *Bibliotheca Sacra*, 142, 565, Jan-Mar 1985, pp. 38-51.

Ginzberg, Louis, *The Legends of the Jews*, Vol. III, trans by Paul Radin, (Philadelphia, Jewish Publication Society of America, 5728-1968).

Ginzburg, Louis, *The Legends of the Jews*, CD-Rom Vol. 2, and Henrietta Szold, trans. Vol. 2, (Baltimore and London, Johns Hopkins University Press, 1998).

Goitein, S.D., *A Mediterranean Society: The Jewish Communities of the Arab World as Portrayed in the Documents of the Cairo Geniza,, Vol. I: Economic Foundations*, (Berkeley, University of California Press, 1967).

Goitein, S.D., *A Mediterranean Society: The Jewish Communities of the Arab World as Portrayed in the Documents of the Cairo Geniza, Vol. III: The Family*, (Berkeley, University of California Press, 1978).

Goitein, S.D., "From Aden to India," in Ranabir Chakravarti (ed.), *Trade in Early India*, (New Delhi, Oxford University Press, 2001), pp. 416-434.

Goitein, S.D., *Jews and Arabs: Their Contacts through the Ages*, (New York, Schocken, 1964).

Goldstein, Bernard, "Astronomy and Astrology in the Works of Abraham Ibn Ezra." in *Arabic Sciences and Philosophy*, Vol. 6, 1996, pp. 9-21.

Goldstein, Bernard, "Astronomy and the Jewish Community in Early Islam," in *Aleph*, Vol. I, 2001, pp. 17-57.

Green, R. Dr. Yosef, e-mail communication 18 July 2005.

Green, Yosef, "The Rebellion of the Bechorim," in *Dor le Dor*, XIV, 2, Winter 1985/86, pp.77-81.

Greene, John T., *Balaam and His Interpreters: A Hermeneutical History of the Balaam Traditions*, (Atlanta, Scholars Press, 1992).

Gross, John, *Shylock: A Legend and Its Legacy*, (New York, Simon and Shuster, 1992).

*The Guide for the Perplexed by Moses Maimonides,* trans. by M. Friedlander, 2$^{nd}$ ed. (New York, Dover, 1904).

*Hirsch Commentary on the Torah,* Vols 1-6, trans by Isaac Levy, (London, Judaica, 1966).

Hoffman, Lawrence A. (ed.), *Traditional Prayers, Modern Commentaries, Vol. 2, The Amidah,* (Woodstock, Vermont, Jewish Lights, 1998).

*Ibn Ezra's Commentary on the Pentateuch: Exodus,* trans and annotated by H. Norman Strickman and Arthur M. Silver, (New York, Menorah, 1996).

*Ibn Ezra's Commentary on the Pentateuch: Genesis,* trans. and annotated by H. Norman Strickman and Arthur M. Silver, (New York, Menorah, 1988).

*Ibn Ezra's Commentary on the Pentateuch: Numbers,* trans. and annotated by H. Norman Strickman and Arthur M. Silver (New York, Menorah, 1999.

*Ibn Ezra's Commentary on the Pentateuch: Deuteronomy,* trans. and annotated by H. Norman Strickman and Arthur M. Silver, (New York, Menorah, 2001.

*Ibn Ezra's Commentary on the Pentateuch: Leviticus,* trans. and annotated by H. Norman Strickman and Arthur M. Silver, (New York, Menorah, 2004).

Idel, Moshe, "The Zodiac in Jewish Thought," in Iris Fishof (ed.) *Written in the Stars: Art and Symbolism of the Zodiac,* (Jerusalem, The Israel Museum, 2001), pp. 20 -27.

Isbell, Charles D., "The Divine Name…as a Symbol of Presence in Israelite Tradition," in *Hebrew Annual Review,* 2, 1978, pp. 101-118).

Isserlin, B.S.J., *The Israelites,* (London, Thames and Hudson, 1998).

Jastrow, Marcus, compiler, *A Dictionary of the Targumim, the Talmud Babli……,* (Jerusalem, 1903, reprinted: Brooklyn, Traditional Press, 1975).

*Jewish Encyclopedia.com,* online information service.

Kalmanofsky, Jeremy, "Sins for the Sake of God," *Conservative Judaism,* 54, 2, Winter 2002, pp. 3-24.

Kellner, M., *Must a Jew Believe Anything?* (London, Littleman Library, 1999),

Levy, B. Barry, "Fixing God's Name," in *The Edah Journal* 12, 2001, Sivan 5761, pp. 1-5.

Leibowitz, Nehama, *Studies in Bamidbar (Numbers),* trans by Aryeh Newman, (Jerusalem, The World Zionist Organization, 5740/1980).

Levine, Baruch A., *The Anchor Bible – Numbers 21 – 36,* translation and commentary, (New York, Doubleday, 2000).

Levy, Leonard W., *Blasphemy: Verbal Offense against the Sacred, from Moses to Salman Rushdie,* (Chapel Hill, University of North Carolina Press, 1993).

Levy, Raphael, *The Astrological Works of Abraham Ibn Ezra,* (Baltimore, Johns Hopkins University, 1927).

Maimonides, Moses, *The Guide for the Perplexed,* trans by M. Friedland, 2nd ed, (New York, Dover, 1956).

Malamud, Bernard, *The Fixer,* (New York, Farrar, Straus, Giroux, 1997).

Mendelsohn, S., *The Criminal Jurisprudence of the Ancient Hebrews,* (Union, New Jersey, The Lawbook Exchange, 1891, reprinted 2001).

*Midrash Rabbah: Genesis,* trans by H. Freedman, (London, New York, Soncino, 1983).

*Midrash Rabbah: Exodus,* trans by S. M. Lehrman, (London, New York, Soncino, 1983).

*Midrash Rabbah: Leviticus* trans by Judah H. Slotkin and J. Israelstam, (London, New York, Soncino, 1983).

*Midrash Rabbah: Numbers,* trans by Judah J. Slotkin, (London, New York, Soncino, 1983).

*Midrash Rabbah: Deuteronomy,* trans by J. Rabbinowitz, (London, New York, Soncino, 1983).

Milgrom, Jacob, trans and commentary, *The JPS Torah Commentary: Numbers,* (Philadelphia, The Jewish Publication Society, 5750/1990).

Milton, John, *Paradise Lost,* Book XII, 645.

Minow, Martha, *Between Vengeance and Forgiveness: Facing History After Genocide and Mass Violence,* (Boston, Beacon, 1998).

Modrzejewsky, Joseph Meleze, *The Jews of Egypt: From Rameses to Emperor Hadrian,* trans by Robert Cornman, (Princeton, Princeton University Press, 1997).

Munk, Elie, *The Call of the Torah: An anthology of interpretation and commentary on the Five Books of Moses – Vayikra,* trans by E. S. Mazer, ed by Yitzchok Kirzner, (Brooklyn, NY, Mesorah), 1992.

Munk, Elie, *The Call of Torah: An anthology of interpretation and commentary on the Five Books of Moses- Bereishis,* trans by E.S. Mazer, (Brooklyn, NY, Mesorah, 1994).

Munk, Elie, *The Call of the Torah: An anthology of interpretation and commentary on the Five Books of Moses-Devarim,* trans by E.S.Mazer, ed by Yitzchok Kirzner, (Brooklyn, NY, Mesorah, 1995).

Munk, Elie, *The Call of the Torah: An anthology of interpretation and commentary on the Five Books of Moses-Bamidbar,* trans by E.S.Mazer, ed by Yitzchok Kirzner, (Brooklyn, NY, Mesorah, 1993).

Munk, Elie, *The Call of the Torah: An anthology of interpretation and commentary on the Five Books of Moses-Shemos,* trans by E. S. Mazer, ed by Yitzchok Kirzner, (Brooklyn, NY, Mesorah, 2001).

Munk, Eliyahu, trans and editor, *Hachut Hameshulash: Commentaries on the Torah,* Vols. 1 - 6, (Jerusalem, Lambda, no date).

Myrick, Kenneth (ed.) *William Shakespeare: The Merchant of Venice,* (New York, A Signet Classic, 1965).

Neusner, Jacob, *A Life of Yohanan Ben Zakkai,* (Leiden, E.J. Brill, 1970).

Neusner, Jacob, trans., *The Tosefta, Vols. I, II,* Peabody,Mass, Hendrickson, 2002).

Onkelos, *The Ariel Chumash,* Vol. I, (Jerusalem, Ariel, 1997).

*Onkelos on the Torah: Understanding the Bible Text –Genesis,* trans and commentary by Israel Drazin and Stanely M. Wagner, (Jersualem, Gefen, 2006/5767).

Peli, Pinchas H., ed. *Soloveitchik on Repentance,* (New York, Paulist Press, 1984).

*Pesikta Rabbati, Vols I and. II,* trans by William G. Braude, Yale Judaica Series, Vol. XVIII, (New Haven, Yale University Press, 1968).

Rakover, Nahum, *Jewish Law in the Debates of the Knesset,* (Jerusalem, The Library of Jewish Law, 1988). pp. 517 – 544. (Hebrew)

*Ramban (Nachmanides) Commentary on the Torah – Genesis,* trans and annotated by Charles B. Chavel, (New York, Shilo, 1971).

*Ramban (Nachmanides) Commentary on the Torah – Exodus,* trans and annotated by Charles B. Chavel, (New York, Shilo, 1973).

*Ramban (Nachmanides) Commentary on the Torah – Leviticus,* trans and annotated by Charles B. Chavel, (New York, Shilo, 1974).

*Ramban (Nachmanides) Commentary on the Torah - Numbers,* trans and annotated by Charles B. Chavel, (New York, Shilo, 1975).

*Ramban (Nachmanides) Commentary on the Torah – Deuteronomy,* trans and annotated by Charles B. Chavel, (New York, Shilo, 1976)

Reeve, Simon, *One Day in September,* (New York, Arcade, 2000).

Rembaum, Joel E., "Regarding the Inclusion of the Names of the Matriarchs in the First Blessing of the Amidah," in *Proceedings of the Committee on Jewish Law and Standards of the Conservative Movement, 1986-1990,* (New York, Rabbinical Assembly, 2001).

Rockaway, Robert, "Hoodlum, Hero, the Jewish Gangster as Defender of His People 1919- 1949" in *American Jewish History,* 82, 1-4, 1994, pp.215-235.

Rosenberg, AJ, editor and translator, *Samuel,* (New York, Judaica, 1991).

*Saadia Gaon: The Book of Beliefs and Opinions,* trans by Samuel Rosenblatt, (New Haven, Yale University Press, 1976).

Schaechter-Haham, Mayer., *Compound of Hebrew in Thousand Stem Words,* (Jerusalem, Kiryat Sefer, 1982).

Schuerer, Emil, *The History of the Jewish People in the Age of Jesus Christ, Vol. II,* revised and edited by Geza Vermes and others, (Edinburgh, T and T Clark, 1979).

Schwarz, Jan, "Death is the only Messiah: Three Supernatural Stories by Yitshok Bashevis," in Seth L. Wolitz (ed.), *The Hidden Isaac Bashevis Singer,* (Austin, Univ. Texas, 2001), p. 107,

*The Secret of the Torah – A Translation of Ibn Ezra's Sefer Yesod...,* trans by H. Norman Strickman, (New Jersey, Jason Aronson, 1995).

Segal, Peretz, "The 'Divine Death Penalty' in the Hatra Inscriptions and the Mishnah," in *Journal of Jewish Studies,* Vol XL, No. 1, Spring 1989, pp. 46-52.

Skehan, Patrick W., "The Divine Name at Qumran, in the Masada Scroll, and in the Septuagint," in the *Bulletin of the International Organization for Septuagint and Cognate Studies,* No. 13, Fall 1980, pp. 14-44.

*Tanakh – The Holy Scriptures: The New JPS Translation According to the Traditional Hebrew Text,* (Philadelphia, New York, The Jewish Publication Society, 5748, 1988).

de Tarragon, Jean-Michel, "Witchcraft, Magic, and Divination in Canaan and Ancient Israel," in Jack M. Sasson, editor in chief, *Civilizations of the Ancient Near East,* Vols. III and IV, (Peabody, Mass, Hendrickson, 1995), pp. 2071-2081.

Tigay, Jeffrey H. "Commentary," in *The JPS Torah Commentary, Deuteronomy,* (Philadelphia, The Jewish Publication Society, 5756, 1996).

*The Tosefta,* Jacob Neusner, trans. (Peabody, Massachusetts, Hendrickson, 2002).

Urbach, Ephraim, *The Halakhah: Its Sources and Development,* trans by Raphael Posner, (Tel Aviv, Modan, 1996).

Urbach, Ephraim E., *The Sages: Their Concepts and Beliefs,* trans by Israel Abrahams, (Jerusalem, Magnes Press, 1975).

Vishny, Paul H., *The Siddur Companion,* (Jerusalem, Devora, 2005).

Weinstein, Brian, "In Defense of Korach," *Jewish Bible Quarterly,* Vol 37, No. 4, 2009, pp. 259-264.

Weinstein, Brian, "Shakespeare's Forgivable Portrayal of Shylock," in *Jewish Bible Quarterly,* Vol. 35, No. 3, 2007, pp. 187-191.

Weinstein, Brian, "Why Exclude Bilhah and Zilpah?"in *CCAR: The Reform Jewish Quarterly,* forthcoming, Winter 2010.

*The Works of Josephus: Complete and Unabridged, New Updated Edition,* trans by William Whiston, (Peabody, Mass, Hendrickson, 1987).